Praise for *The PRT Pocket Guide*

"An outstanding volume...very user friendly, highly informative, and immensely practical. It is a valuable addition to the library of anyone who works with children with autism." —**Fred Volkmar, M.D.,** Director, Child Study Center, and Professor, Yale University School of Medicine

"This guide is a must-have....It describes an intervention that is not only logical, but proven. Prescribed ways to interact with one's child require patience and practice. There is no magic bullet, but...PRT offers true help and hope." —**Howard Taras, M.D.,** School District Physician Consultant and Professor of Pediatrics, University of California–San Diego

"Provides practical and essential information for all service providers. It's a source I will definitely refer to over and over again." —**Joan Hersh, M.A.,** Teacher, Preschool Blended Program, Fountain Valley School District, California

"Among the best books I've read on naturalistic intervention strategies based on evidence-based practices. Immensely readable with oodles of concrete examples and great illustrations, while strongly rooted in solid scientific principles. A gem from Bob and Lynn Koegel." —**Travis Thompson, Ph.D.,** University of Minnesota

"Lynn and Robert Koegel are by far the most authoritative voices in the field of autism diagnosis and treatment. Their long-awaited book on PRT is a must-read for parents and professionals caring for children with autism spectrum disorders." —**Areva D. Martin, Esq.,** Founder and President, Special Needs Network, Inc.; author of *The Everyday Advocate: Standing Up for Your Child with Autism or Other Special Needs*

"A pivotal book on PRT...translate[s] scientific and clinical evidence into practical procedures that practitioners and parents will find meaningful and effective." —**Samuel L. Odom, Ph.D.,** Director, FPG Child Development Institute, University of North Carolina at Chapel Hill

"A highly accessible and imminently practical description of PRT and its use in everyday settings. Through multiple and compelling examples of the effective use of PRT in home, school, and community settings, the authors bring to life the key components of this well-established, evidence-based approach." —**Joseph M. Lucyshyn, Ph.D., BCBA,** University of British Columbia, Vancouver

"Step-by-step guidance through the treatment process, enhanced by examples and anecdotes from real life. It is a practical, user-friendly resource." —**Anna Burke,** Coordinator, Cape Breton Community Respite, Society for Treatment of Autism, Sydney, Nova Scotia

"Provides an insider's view of Bob and Lynn Koegel's pioneering work with children on the autism spectrum. A terrific guide that will be immensely popular among parents, teachers, and others." —**V. Mark Durand, Ph.D.,** Professor of Psychology, University of South Florida St. Petersburg; co-editor, *Journal of Positive Behavior Interventions*

"Pivotal Response Treatment was instrumental in helping my son become the successful, independent college student he is today. Filled with practical procedures and real-life examples, this concise, approachable book is the perfect guide for family and team members." —**Claire LaZebnik,** author of *Family and Other Nonreturnable Gifts*; coauthor of *Overcoming Autism* and *Growing Up on the Spectrum*

"By far the clearest, most usable, and most engaging description of PRT produced to date. Kudos to the Koegels for giving us a hugely valuable book that will be a treasure for all families and professionals affected by autism." —**Glen Dunlap, Ph.D.,** University of South Florida and University of Nevada, Reno

"PRT is based on decades of solid research demonstrating that it is possible to produce 'big gains without pain' in the treatment of children with autism. In this easy-to-read summary of the key elements of PRT, the Koegels have demonstrated once again that they understand both children with autism and the important role their family members play in intervention." —**Pat Mirenda, Ph.D., BCBA-D,** Professor, Department of Educational & Counselling Psychology and Special Education, University of British Columbia, Vancouver

The PRT Pocket Guide

Pivotal Response Treatment for Autism Spectrum Disorders

by

Robert L. Koegel, Ph.D.

and

Lynn Kern Koegel, Ph.D.

Koegel Autism Center
University of California, Santa Barbara

with invited contributor

·P·A·U·L·H·
BROOKES
PUBLISHING CO®

Baltimore • London • Sydney

Paul H. Brookes Publishing Co.
Post Office Box 10624
Baltimore, Maryland 21285-0624
www.brookespublishing.com

Typeset by Network Publishing Partners, Inc., Glenview, Illinois.
Manufactured in the United States of America by
Versa Press, Inc., East Peoria, Illinois.

Photograph on the cover copyright © istockphoto.com. As applicable, other photos are
used by permission of the individuals pictured and/or their parents/guardians.

The individuals described in this book are composites or real people whose situations are
masked and are based on the authors' experiences. In all instances, names and identifying
details have been changed to protect confidentiality.

Library of Congress Cataloging-in-Publication Data

Koegel, Robert L., 1944-
   The PRT pocket guide : pivotal response treatment for autism spectrum disorders / by
Robert L. Koegel and Lynn Kern Koegel ; with invited contributor, Sarah Kuriakose.
     p.   cm.
   Includes bibliographical references and index.
   ISBN-13: 978-1-59857-105-9 (perfect (pbk.)
   ISBN-10: 1-59857-105-2 (perfect (pbk.)
   1. Autism—Treatment.   I. Koegel, Lynn Kern.   II. Kuriakose, Sarah.   III. Title.
RC553.A88K63 2012
616.85'882—dc23   2011052957

British Library Cataloguing in Publication data are available from the British Library.

2016   2015   2014   2013   2012
10   9   8   7   6   5   4   3   2   1

Contents

About the Authors

Robert L. Koegel, Ph.D., has focused his career in the area of autism, specializing in language intervention, family support, and school inclusion. Dr. Robert L. Koegel is Director of the Koegel Autism Center at the University of California, Santa Barbara. He has published more than 200 articles and papers relating to the treatment of autism, has published six books on the treatment of autism and positive behavioral support, and is Editor of the *Journal of Positive Behavior Interventions.* Models of his procedures have been used in public schools and in parent education programs throughout the United States and in other countries. He has trained many health care and special education leaders in the United States and abroad.

Lynn Kern Koegel, Ph.D., is Director of Clinical Services at the Koegel Autism Center and Director of the Eli and Edythe L. Broad Center for Asperger's Research. She has been active in the development of programs to improve communication in children with autism, including the development of first words, grammatical structures, pragmatics, and social conversation. In addition to her published books and articles in the area of communication and language development, Dr. Lynn Kern Koegel has developed and published procedures and field manuals in the area of self-management and functional analysis that are used in school districts and by parents throughout the United States and have been translated into other major languages. Dr. Lynn Kern Koegel is the author of *Overcoming Autism: Finding the Answers, Strategies, and Hope that Can Transform a Child's Life* (Viking/Penguin, 2004) and *Growing Up on the Spectrum* (Viking/Penguin, 2009) with Claire LaZebnik.

The Koegels are the developers of Pivotal Response Treatment, which focuses on motivation. They were the recipients of the first annual Children's Television Workshop Sesame Street Award for brightening the lives of children and the first annual Autism Speaks award for science and research. In addition, Dr. Lynn Kern Koegel appeared on ABC's hit show *Supernanny,* working with a child with autism. The University of California, Santa Barbara, received a $2.35 million gift to expand the physical space of the Autism Research and Training Center, which was renamed the Koegel Autism Center in recognition of the Koegels' work on behalf of children with autism, and a large gift from the Eli and Edythe L. Broad Foundation to start a center for Asperger syndrome research, which is now part of the Koegel Autism Center.

For the Reader

If you're interested in learning more about PRT®, the authors and their team offer a range of resources, services, and training. Please see their web site, http://www.koegelautism.com, for more information or to schedule an event. Also note that PRT®, Pivotal Response Teaching®, Pivotal Response Training®, and Pivotal Response Treatment® are registered service marks with the U.S. Patent and Trademark Office, registered as marks of Koegel Autism Consultants, LLC, in association with educational conferences and workshops the authors provide in the field of non-aversive treatment interventions for children with autism and with the authors' learning center.

Another good resource for detailed information is the authors' earlier book *Pivotal Response Treatments for Autism: Communication, Social, & Academic Development*, also published by Paul H. Brookes Publishing Co.

Preface

This book is designed to be an accessible and practical guide describing Pivotal Response Treatment (PRT) for autism and Asperger syndrome. The book explains, in an easy-to-follow and practical manner, what PRT is and what its key underlying features are, including the importance of family involvement and intervention in everyday settings. Specifically, it explains how to focus on core, keystone areas, called pivotal areas, which produce extremely widespread and rapid treatment gains. In addition, we give detailed descriptions of the scientific evidence that supports each component of PRT and the overall PRT package.

In each chapter we provide poignant vignettes—composite and masked real examples—from our own practice that illustrate the essential points. Each chapter also includes a discussion of the science that provides a foundation for the points described. Following the scientific background, we offer several practical and helpful examples of how to implement the intervention with children of different levels of functioning, ranging from those with more significant needs to individuals diagnosed with Asperger syndrome, who have their own unique support needs. These sections are called "Making It Work in Everyday Settings." When providing treatment in everyday settings, things aren't as simple as they seem on paper, so that's why we've tried to help you figure out how to apply the interventions while navigating the unexpected circumstances that seem to come up constantly in the real world.

We hope this book will become a practical guide for parents, relatives, teachers, and practitioners who interact regularly with individuals with autism and who also want to be assured that the interventions they are using are supported by empirical evidence. And even if you aren't working directly with a child on the autism spectrum—for example, if you are a legislator, principal, special education administrator, attorney, or other professional whose work intersects the world of autism—we hope you'll also come to understand the importance of practical and scientifically sound interventions such as PRT.

Acknowledgments

We appreciate the assistance of Kristen Ashbaugh, who helped greatly with the editorial process in the development of this book. As always, we would like to acknowledge the families of the children with whom we work, who are a major inspiration to us. We are also grateful for the assistance of the funding agencies that have made possible much of the research described in this book. A great deal of our research has been funded by grants awarded by the California Children and Families Commission, the California State Council on Developmental Disabilities, the National Institute on Disability and Rehabilitation Research, the National Institute of Mental Health, the National Institutes of Health, the U.S. Department of Education, and the U.S. Public Health Service.

Introduction

Pivotal Response Treatment (PRT) is one of the few evidence-based approaches for the treatment of autism. That is, the approach is supported by research that meets the standards set by many professional agencies and organizations, such as the American Psychological Association. That's important because supporting children and families affected by autism is a race against time. Families can't afford to repeatedly go up blind alleys with treatment procedures that sound good but have no evidence to support their effectiveness in helping children with autism. Each day more children are diagnosed with autism, and they need instruction and intervention in many different areas. Furthermore, early intervention is effective—partly because it keeps bad habits from getting started (habits that would be hard to break), but also because without intervention kids on the autism spectrum get worse, whereas with intervention they get better. Although it's never too late, the earlier any communication delays and social challenges are addressed, the sooner parents, teachers, and therapists can start helping the kids learn what they'll need to survive and thrive.

PRT focuses on core underlying areas that are critical for children with autism. Functionally, the major core area—which affects all other areas—is motivation to engage in social communication. That core area is linked both to underlying neurological bases and to thousands of individual behaviors that are affected by the motivational problem as the children develop. The figure on the next page shows the many interrelationships addressed by PRT.

It's also important to understand that the PRT procedures were developed over many, many years and that there are now hundreds of studies showing their effectiveness. PRT is based on behavioral intervention, a method developed in earlier work in the field of applied behavior analysis that is also supported by plenty of research that documents its effectiveness as an approach for autism. In general, for all behavioral interventions, the standards for documenting treatment effectiveness require multiple research studies

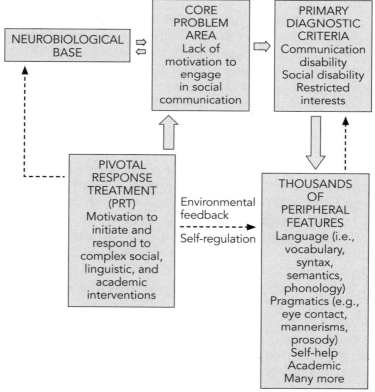

A model of pivotal response intervention.

conducted by several independent researchers using either randomized, controlled experimental designs or rigorous single-case experimental designs, or both. (See Chambless & Ollendick, 2001, for a general description of these standards.) In short, this means that not only have we succeeded with research conducted in our own clinics, but that other researchers, working in other clinics and using a variety of different experimental designs, have also found the same positive results. This duplication shows that there isn't bias on our part. It really works.

Another important point is that not only has the PRT "package" been shown to make real and significant changes, but every component of PRT has also been tested individually and found to be valuable in intervention (see R.L. Koegel, Koegel, & Camarata, 2010; R.L. Koegel, Koegel, Vernon, & Brookman-Frazee, 2010; National Autism Center, 2009; National Research Council, 2001; Odom, Boyd, Hall, & Hume, 2010a, 2010b; Simpson, 2005). As we'll repeat many times in this book, there are a lot of packaged autism interventions out there—some we've all heard of—for which the proponents haven't shown that the individual components work. Using those interventions may be wasting valuable time teaching behaviors that just aren't helpful for the child.

It's important to note that because PRT is scientifically based, it continues to evolve, with new components being added as they are discovered. This point is critical, because all the answers aren't in yet, and there are always improvements that can be made. As new ways to teach or to teach more effectively are found—so the kids will learn faster and have more fun—the methods will continue to change. As an example, as the PRT approach has been developed and refined over the years, it has gone by several different names. When it was first applied specifically to communication, as in the original studies focused on teaching first words, it was called the "Natural Language Paradigm," or NLP for short. It got that name because the motivational components incorporated into the treatment for communication resembled natural interactions with children, as opposed to the more structured, drill-type interventions that were commonly used at that time.

Through further research, it became clear that the approach was surprisingly effective in many areas beyond communication. Thus, the approach began to go by the name "Pivotal Response Treatment" to reflect its impact on thousands of behaviors within the overall condition of autism. The table summarizes the evidence supporting the comprehensive PRT package.

There are four primary reasons why empirical evidence is important when choosing which treatment approach to use.

1. Empirical evidence separates approaches that really work from approaches that are mere fantasy and hype or are simply less effective. Don't be fooled by fancy brochures and treatment providers claiming to have the "latest and greatest" interventions for autism. That's unlikely. Because nonscientific approaches may sound good on paper or in dramatic speeches by celebrities, one can be easily deceived by rhetoric and fancy sales pitches.

2. Certifying agencies, as well as credentialing and licensing bodies, are increasingly requiring professionals to use approaches that are backed by sound scientific evidence, making those who use non–evidence-based approaches increasingly vulnerable to lawsuits. Don't get caught in that situation, as you'll look extremely ill informed in court.

3. Insurance companies and other third-party funding agencies are refusing to pay for treatments that do not have scientific evidence to back their effectiveness. It may sound superficial, but someone has to pay for the treatment, and no one wants to pay for something that doesn't work!

Summarized empirical support for Pivotal Response Treatment (PRT)

Study	Title	Notable treatment outcome(s)
Original PRT studies		
R.L. Koegel, O'Dell, and Koegel (1987)	A Natural Language Paradigm for Teaching Nonverbal Autistic Children	Children produced more imitative and spontaneous utterances in PRT condition than in traditional discrete trial training. Generalization of treatment gains occurred only in PRT condition.
R.L. Koegel, Koegel, and Surratt (1992)	Language Intervention and Disruptive Behavior in Preschool Children with Autism	Increased language responding and fewer disruptive behaviors occurred during the PRT condition compared to traditional discrete trial training.
L.K. Koegel, Koegel, Shoshan, and McNerney (1999), Phase 1	Pivotal Response Intervention II: Preliminary Long-Term Outcome Data	Looking through retrospective analysis, children with poor and favorable outcomes had comparable language ages and adaptive behavior scale scores at preintervention, but children who exhibited high levels of spontaneous initiations at preintervention had more favorable outcomes.
L.K. Koegel, Koegel, Shoshan, and McNerney (1999), Phase 2	Pivotal Response Intervention II: Preliminary Long-Term Outcome Data	Following PRT initiation training, children increased their adaptive and pragmatic scores to near chronological age level. They did not retain their diagnosis of autism or their special education placements. Social/academic functioning was comparable to that of typically developing peers.
L.K. Koegel, Carter, and Koegel (2003)	Teaching Children with Autism Self-Initiations as a Pivotal Response	Through PRT, children were successfully taught to use the queries "What happened?" or "What's happening?" during intervention. Children generalized the use of -ing and -ed to other verbs and increased their mean length of utterance and verb diversity.
R.L. Koegel, Shirotova, and Koegel (2009b)	Brief Report: Using Individualized Orienting Cues to Facilitate First-Word Acquisition in Non-responders with Autism	PRT with individualized orienting cues produced verbal communication gains in correct responding, correct phonemes, and independent word production that PRT without such cues did not.

(continued)

Summarized empirical support for Pivotal Response Treatment (PRT) (continued)

Study	Title	Notable treatment outcome(s)
R.L. Koegel, Vernon, and Koegel (2009)	Improving Social Initiations in Young Children with Autism Using Reinforcers with Embedded Social Interactions	PRT with embedded social interactions resulted in increased levels of child-initiated social engagement during communication, improved nonverbal dyadic orienting, and higher ratings of overall child affect compared to the nonembedded conditions.

Independent replications of PRT effectiveness with original lab collaboration

Study	Title	Notable treatment outcome(s)
Schreibman, Kaneko, and Koegel (1991)	Positive Affect of Parents of Autistic Children: A Comparison Across Two Teaching Techniques	Parents trained in PRT were observed displaying significantly more positive affect than parents trained in discrete trial training.
R.L. Koegel, Bimbela, and Schreibman (1996)	Collateral Effects of Parent Training on Family Interactions	Discrete trial condition resulted in no significant influence on interactions, while PRT resulted in positive parent–child interactions noted on ratings of happiness, interest, stress, and communication style during dinnertime probes.
R.L. Koegel, Camarata, Koegel, Ben-Tall, and Smith (1998)	Increasing Speech Intelligibility in Children with Autism	Significant gains observed in correct production of target sounds and speech intelligibility during the PRT intervention.
L.K. Koegel, Camarata, Valdez-Menchaca, and Koegel (1998)	Setting Generalization of Question-Asking by Children with Autism	Children learned in PRT to consistently and spontaneously initiate "What's that?" across treatment and generalization settings. Significant increase in vocabulary achieved due to item label acquisition.
Bryson et al. (2007)	Large Scale Dissemination and Community Implementation of Pivotal Response Treatment: Program Description and Preliminary Data	Preliminary data show that PRT providers who participated in large-scale, community training maintained fidelity of implementation across treatment time and increased the functional verbal utterances of the participant children.

Nefdt, Koegel, Singer, and Gerber (2010)	The Use of a Self-Directed Learning Program to Provide Introductory Training in Pivotal Response Treatment to Parents of Children with Autism	The majority of parents participating in the PRT Self-Directed Learning Program (DVD and accompanying materials) completed the program, demonstrated learning of specified procedures, and was observed to appear more confident during parent–child interactions.

Independent replications of effectiveness of PRT

Laski, Charlop-Christy, and Schreibman (1988)	Training Parents to Use the Natural Language Paradigm to Increase Their Autistic Children's Speech	After parent training in PRT at home and in a clinic setting, posttreatment increases in parent requests for vocalizations were observed, as were increases in children's verbal responsiveness during intervention and generalization.
Pierce and Schreibman (1995)	Increasing Complex Play in Children with Autism via Peer-Implemented Pivotal Response Training	Following peer-implemented PRT, children increased interactions to a high level of intervals and increased play and conversation initiations. Children exhibited increases in coordinated and supported joint attention behaviors following treatment.
Thorp, Stahmer, and Schreibman (1995)	Effects of Sociodramatic Play Training on Children with Autism	All children increased in all play behavior measures following PRT teaching of sociodramatic play. Play behavior gains maintained during generalization.
Stahmer (1995)	Teaching Symbolic Play to Children with Autism Using Pivotal Response Training	Modified PRT using symbolic play as a target behavior increased symbolic play and play complexity. Treatment gains were maintained during generalizations across toys, settings, and partners.
Pierce and Schreibman (1997)	Multiple Peer Use of Pivotal Response Training Social Behaviors of Classmates with Autism: Results from Trained and Untrained Peers	Peer-implemented PRT was successful in producing positive social behavior change across multiple peer implementers. The social behavior change was maintained during generalization with untrained peers.

(continued)

Summarized empirical support for Pivotal Response Treatment (PRT) *(continued)*

Study	Title	Notable treatment outcome(s)
Sherer and Schreibman (2005)	Individual Behavioral Profiles and Predictors of Treatment Effectiveness for Children with Autism	Children profiled as predicted responders to PRT exhibited increases in language, play, and social behavior following PRT intervention.
Baker-Ericzén, Stahmer, and Burns (2007)	Child Demographics Associated with Outcomes in a Community-Based Pivotal Response Training Program	Following a 12-week PRT parent education program, all children showed significant improvement in adaptive behavior scale scores regardless of gender, age, and race/ethnicity of the children/families.
Vismara and Lyons (2007)	Using Perseverative Interests to Elicit Joint Attention Behaviors in Young Children with Autism: Theoretical and Clinical Implications for Understanding Motivation	Using the child's perseverative interests in a PRT model increased joint attention initiations.
Gillett and LeBlanc (2007)	Parent-Implemented Natural Language Paradigm to Increase Language and Play in Children with Autism	Parent-implemented PRT led to increases in overall rate and spontaneity of utterances for children. Children also showed an increase in appropriate play. Parents rated the intervention simple to implement and endorsed continued use of PRT.
Harper, Symon, and Frea (2008)	Recess Is Time-In: Using Peers to Improve Social Skills of Children with Autism	Peer implementation of PRT increased initiations and turn-taking initiations.

4. Serious problems can occur when approaches that have not been properly tested are employed: In addition to wasting the children's valuable time, untested procedures are often found to be risky or dangerous, and using them may create problems that are greater than the original symptoms of autism. Take the casein-free diet, for example. Many parents put their children on this diet, only to find that it results in low bone density after several years—and studies now show that it doesn't help the symptoms of autism. In short, remember that evidence-based procedures are essential, valuable, and available. *Beware of snake-oil salesmen!*

This book presents scientifically based and practical intervention procedures that can be implemented in everyday settings; are easy and fun to implement; and produce valuable treatment gains for children with autism, as well as benefits for the entire family's lifestyle. PRT has been used effectively for more than 25 years with hundreds of thousands of families. By focusing on several foundational areas of development in children, PRT results in life-changing improvements for children with an autism diagnosis. The following chapters will highlight each of the pivotal areas and provide details on effective implementation and expected outcomes.

I

What Is the P in PRT?

1

Treatment of Pivotal Areas

Nathan is 4 and was diagnosed with autism just before his third birthday. It took his parents about four months following his diagnosis to secure services from a reputable agency that provided applied behavior analysis (ABA) intervention. At first, the ABA therapists taught Nathan how to sit (and remain sitting) in a chair, which was wonderful for his parents, as he had never sat for more than 10 or 20 seconds, even during meals. At the beginning of intervention, Nathan cried whenever the therapists arrived. In fact, he started crying when he heard one of their cars making its way up the driveway. He ran frantically from window to window, distressed and upset, crying and whining all the while. After about four months, he began to appear resigned to the fact that they would visit daily, although his face definitely showed symptoms of discomfort. After he had learned how to sit, the therapists began working on imitation, first nonverbal, by saying "Do this!" while demonstrating a gross motor movement, and then verbal. After receiving services for slightly more than a year, Nathan had made slow but steady progress. He could sit for most of the 6 hours on days when he got intervention (with short breaks every half hour or so), and he was able to imitate motor movements and say about 30 words. Nathan's parents adored his therapists and were delighted that he no longer engaged in disruptive behavior. However, they were worried about his slow progress and his apparent unease during the sessions. For these reasons, they called us at the Koegel Autism Center at the University of California, Santa Barbara (UCSB), looking for something more.

To understand the problems in Nathan's intervention, consider the following. To receive a diagnosis of autism, a child has to exhibit deficits in many areas, including communication, socialization, and a variety of interests. It boils down to needing a lot of intervention. On top of that, if a child has difficulty with communication, he or she may get frustrated and develop other behaviors, such as aggression or self-injury. And if socialization is difficult, the child may not be observing peers and getting feedback from them—which is so critical to fitting in. Careful monitoring of these symptoms is important, and it's never too soon to start. The Measurement: Baseline and Responsiveness to Intervention Guide form in this chapter provides a checklist that can be used to collect a baseline of a child's symptoms before intervention begins.

Now, let's continue with some history. Not too many years ago children with autism were considered "uneducable," and by adolescence most were institutionalized. Before the 1960s, none of the interventions for children with autism were based on any science. In the 1960s, researchers began looking for ways to help such children. The early work focused primarily on consequences, and, unfortunately, many children were the recipients of harsh and sometimes painful consequences. Along with such consequences, the children received praise and tangible rewards (usually small edibles) for exhibiting appropriate behavior. Although this approach worked and the children improved with these types of interventions, progress was slow—really slow—and the kids never really seemed to enjoy the sessions. In fact, many spent a good part of the session trying to escape—crying, screaming, kicking, and biting! On top of that, the treatment was long, tedious, and laborious for both the clinician and the child. Curricula were lengthy, and thousands of target behaviors were addressed.

From what you know about children on the spectrum, you can imagine why this intervention made sense back then. First and foremost, communication is difficult for a child with autism. Very difficult. So is socialization. For those reasons, it is unlikely that the child will approach you, ask you questions, and want to get your attention for every little thing, no matter how small or insignificant, like a typically developing child does. In contrast, the child is more likely to be content playing alone, and he may risk his life trying to get something off a top shelf rather than trying to ask for help. In the early days of autism interventions, because the children were difficult to teach, were not social, and appeared unmotivated, the researchers attempted to figure out ways to get a child's attention and improve responsiveness. They attempted to do this through a very structured, artificial interaction.

Specifically, in the 1960s very structured programs were developed with one-on-one interventionists. Although these new methods were more effective than previous, non–evidence-based attempts to work with these children, improvements still came slowly. The procedures were implemented in environments that were very free of distractions, and the first thing a therapist did was try to get the child's attention. This was usually accomplished by seating the child in a small chair directly in front of the therapist, who kept saying to him "Look at me." As soon as the child looked, the therapist immediately said "Good job!" or made some other positive comment and gave the child a small treat—an M&M, potato chip, peanut, or other tasty tidbit. Once the child was looking or paying attention, the therapist started working on behaviors. The therapist usually started with trying to get the child to imitate. For example, the therapist would say "Do this" while raising her hands high up above her head. If the child imitated, the therapist patted him on the tummy and gave him the verbal and edible reward. If he didn't respond, the therapist might have another adult sit behind the child and physically prompt

Measurement: Baseline and Responsiveness to Intervention Guide

Symptom area	Check level	Define behavior	Measure amount of behavior	When/where is the behavior absent/present
1. Communication				
Nonverbal *Verbal attempts* *Sounds*	☐☐			
Words				
Combines words *Two-word combinations* *Combinations of three or more words* *Conversational*	☐☐			
2. Social				
Plays alone				
Plays repetitively with toys				
Plays appropriately with toys				
Plays with peers				
Make-believe play				

Symptom area	Check level	Define behavior	Measure amount of behavior	When/where is the behavior absent/present
3. Interests				
Limited interests				
Inflexible				
Repetitive behaviors *Without objects* *With objects*	☐			
4. Disruptive behavior				
Crying				
Tantrums				
Self-injury				
Aggression				
Property destruction				

him to imitate. Gradually and systematically, the prompts were faded out until the child imitated the therapist by himself. And so it went, teaching behavior after behavior.

After the child could imitate many physical behaviors, the therapist started on communication, trying to get the child to imitate a sound, such as "mmmm." As with the physical imitation, if the child responded, the therapist gave him verbal praise and a treat, and if he didn't respond, the therapist would provide a physical prompt, such as holding his lips together. Once the child was repeating the sound reliably, the therapist added another sound, such as "ahhh." At that point the therapist's goal was to get the child to distinguish the difference between the "mmmm" and the "ahhh," so the therapist varied those sounds back and forth until the child knew the difference. Next, the therapist tried putting the two sounds together. To do this, the therapist had the child say "mmmm" and then "ahhh" over and over again, while prompting for the sounds to be said closer and closer together until the child was eventually saying "ma." Next, the therapist prompted the child to put the syllable together twice so that the child was saying "mama." Aha! A first word, *finally*, after all that work! Unfortunately, even though the child had said a word, he didn't know what it meant.

You can see how long and laborious teaching each task was. And you can see why, given those early methods, the children made very slow progress. But you have to remember that this was a few decades back, when many people said these kids were "uneducable" and couldn't learn. Although the procedures were painfully slow and laborious, the kids *did* learn, and that was a whole lot better than giving up on them. Yet something still seemed to be wrong.

One day we were brainstorming about how long it took to teach each behavior, and we were also thinking about how typically developing kids just sort of "pick up" the behaviors without having to be specifically taught every single one. Bob remarked that the kids with autism just didn't seem "motivated" to learn. And that's what started a whole long line of research. As shown in the diagram about the development of Pivotal Response Treatment (PRT), ideas progressed from the early days of structured discrete trial training to understanding that the children's lack of motivation to com-

1960s — Start of structured discrete trial training
(Hewett, 1965; Lovaas, Berberich, Perloff, & Schaeffer, 1966; Sloane & MacAulay, 1968; Wolf, Risley, & Mees, 1964)

1973 — Still unable to find a pivotal behavior
(Lovaas, Koegel, Simmons, & Long, 1973)

1979 — Start of focus on motivation as critical
(R.L. Koegel & Egel, 1979)

1980s — Research on individual components of PRT
(Dunlap, 1984; Dunlap & Koegel, 1980; R.L. Koegel, Dyer, & Bell, 1987; R.L. Koegel & Koegel, 2006; R.L. Koegel, Koegel, & Surratt, 1992; R.L. Koegel, O'Dell, & Dunlap, 1988; R.L. Koegel, O'Dell, & Koegel, 1987; R.L. Koegel & Williams, 1980; Williams, Koegel, & Egel, 1981)

1985 — More intense discussion of motivation as critical
(R.L. Koegel & Mentis, 1985)

1987 — Start of PRT (Natural Language Paradigm)
(R.L. Koegel, O'Dell, & Koegel, 1987)

1988 — First discussion of pivotal areas being effective in treatment
(R.L. Koegel & Koegel, 1988)

Development of Pivotal Response Treatment (PRT).

municate was a serious core problem that led to enormous numbers of "side effects." Here was the big, daunting question: How do you motivate kids with autism? How do you make them *want* to learn? At that time we really didn't know. In fact, we didn't even know how to define "motivation."

So we began our quest to find the key to motivation and to figure out what would spark an interest in the kids we worked with. We had the same concern that Nathan's parents had: Even if the children were making gains, if they weren't also enjoying the intervention, something was seriously wrong.

Our answers started coming in slowly. We worked from all angles: How were we presenting the instruction? What materials were we using? How were we rewarding the children? As we searched, we began finding areas that seemed to help the children learn faster and that helped us move away from needing to teach each individual behavior, one at time, by using a drill format that required the children to sit for many hours, much as the therapists were doing with Nathan. We shifted our approach by trying to define "pivotal" areas: domains of behavior that, once taught, would have a positive effect on all types of other behaviors. We *needed* to do this to help the children make more rapid progress—or even overcome all their symptoms—and that wouldn't be possible if we had to work one behavior at a time. It would just take way too long.

So there you have it. That's why we began our pursuit of pivotal behaviors. There had to be a better way. It's important to remember that getting science into the "real world" is a slow process. They say it can take up to 20 years—yes, 20—from the time a discovery is made until it is actively used in everyday life. That's why it's so important for parents like Nathan's to keep up with the latest research and to ensure that their children are getting the most up-to-date interventions.

THE SCIENCE BEHIND THE
APPLIED BEHAVIOR ANALYSIS AND
PIVOTAL RESPONSE TREATMENT METHODS

Before the 1960s, "treatment" for autism was a sad thing for everyone because most of the treatments were based on the outdated parental-causation theory. Concerned parents were told that the best thing they could do for their child was to institutionalize him or her and get themselves into therapy for their own shortcomings. Even parents who decided to keep their child at home often had to institutionalize the child eventually, in adolescence or young adulthood. Without any good interventions, the child's disruptive behaviors got beyond what the parents could control. Fortunately, many systematic interventions are now available for individuals with autism. These interventions can reduce problem behaviors, improve communication, help children and adults learn to socialize, and expand their interests. However, most of them focus on individual target behaviors. Although there is nothing wrong with this strategy, and a child will make improvements when the interventionist works on individual behaviors, it takes time. Lots of time. And that's expensive and slow. And even if you have money, time is a different matter. No one wants his or her child to improve slowly. For that reason, we continued searching for pivotal areas that might be effective in making faster and more substantial improvements. By "pivotal areas" we mean behaviors that, when taught, would result in improvements in thousands of other behaviors that are among the symptoms of autism. Simply stated, there are too many behaviors that require intervention. If the goal is for the child to lose all the symptoms of autism, addressing behaviors one at a time simply takes too long. If pivotal behaviors could be identified, the likelihood of widespread, fluidly integrated improvements seemed attainable.

This goal was addressed early on by Dr. Robert Koegel's mentor, Ivar Lovaas (e.g., Lovaas, Berberich, Perloff, & Schaeffer, 1966; Lovaas, Schaeffer, & Simmons, 1965), who focused on imitation and social behavior, speculating that if those areas could be improved, they would provide a basic mechanism for typical child development. That made perfect sense. The idea was that once the children became social and imitated their peers, they should show rapid and widespread improvement throughout their lives. The problem was figuring out how to teach those skills. It wasn't easy to teach the children to imitate, and, even when they were successfully taught, getting them to show any generalized imitation, let alone generalized interest in other people, just didn't happen. Eventually, Lovaas made some major breakthroughs showing that, to some extent, the children could learn to generalize their imitation skills and become more social. Yet the type of generalization necessary to produce gains in untreated areas was still elusive (Lovaas et al., 1965; Lovaas et al., 1966). Thus, at that time, it seemed as though neither imitation nor social behavior was a pivotal area for autism. Lovaas and many of us on his team of graduate students continued for many years to try to identify pivotal areas, always without success. In the 1970s, Lovaas, Koegel, Simmons, and Long (1973) suggested that it might be impossible to identify any pivotal behavior for this population.

So the focus on individual target behaviors continued, with thousands of teaching trials being necessary to make gains. And this took time and effort—many, many hours a week with many, many trials on each target behavior. Teaching was conducted primarily through what became known as an intensive discrete trial model. In this model, the therapist provided a prompt, waited for the child to respond, then gave a consequence (thus it was also described as the A-B-C—antecedent, behavior, consequence—procedure). Again, this intervention was successful, leading to large improvements in many individual behaviors, with major improvements in the overall condition of autism (see Lovaas, 1987). It's just that the work was very laborious, both for interventionists and for the children themselves. Often the children would become disruptive in an attempt to avoid the very demanding trials, which created a new problem. Getting rid of the disruptive behaviors required some type of consequence, and so researchers began studying the effectiveness of using punishment. Thus, a vicious cycle began: The treatment was demanding and unpleasant—the children got disruptive—the children got punished. As the field moved increasingly toward an emphasis on early intervention, this extremely demanding, intensive, and frequently punishment-dependent approach took its toll, and many people were concerned about the stress it might be placing on the children and their families.

Thus, in the late 1970s and 1980s, a group of us at UCSB began to search further for pivotal areas. This time we made some breakthroughs. We found some key areas that produced widespread improvement in the children's functioning with much less effort required on the part of the children, their parents, or their interventionists, compared to the earlier discrete trial approach that focused on individual target behaviors. This made a huge difference. The children learned faster, the intervention was easier for families to learn, and it was much easier than targeting the individual behaviors, so many more clinicians stayed in the field. In short, the introduction of what is now known as Pivotal Response Treatment made an enormous difference for everyone. There is now a large body of research showing that specific pivotal areas are critical for children with autism. These studies, numbering in the hundreds and performed both within and outside our labs, have documented the effectiveness of targeting pivotal areas in at least three different ways. First, studies have proven how important pivotal responses are for improving many, many behaviors, including academics, play, socialization, language acquisi-

CHANGING PIVOTAL AREAS CHANGES MANY OTHER AREAS	
Academics	Engagement
Play	First words
Social behavior	Homework completion
Language	Mathematics
Communication	Reading

Areas affected by Pivotal Response Treatment (PRT).

tion, communication, engagement, first words, homework completion, mathematics, reading, and so forth.

Second, studies have shown that there are several different pivotal areas and that specific pivotal intervention packages (e.g., a motivational package, a self-initiations package) are wildly effective in producing widespread and long-term improvements. Third, research has examined the effectiveness of PRT when used as a comprehensive package across the many different activities a child participates in throughout the day and across many different settings, such as school, home, and community settings. In short, many studies document that PRT is more efficient, effective, and helpful overall for children with autism and their families compared to previous interventions; that it works with many different behaviors; and that it generalizes across settings. Those are the reasons why we have worked so hard to target these pivotal areas.

Motivation

The very first pivotal area we discovered was motivation. The earliest hints that there might be a pivotal area of motivation came in a research study we conducted comparing periods of steady streams of correct responding with periods of responding in which there were lots of incorrect

This child can learn concepts such as "fast," "slow," "high," and "low" by employing the natural reinforcer he achieves through playing ball.

responses (R.L. Koegel & Egel, 1979; R.L. Koegel & Mentis, 1985). We noticed that the children became far more motivated to continue learning when they were having steady periods of success. This discovery led to research on the development of the powerful motivational package that was eventually named PRT. We conducted the earliest study on the motivational package in 1987 (R.L. Koegel, O'Dell, & Koegel, 1987). In this experiment, we showed that discrete trial intervention could be improved dramatically when specific motivational variables (e.g., child's choice of stimulus materials, use of natural reinforcers) were incorporated into the intervention procedures. In this study we weren't trying to say that there was anything wrong with discrete trials. In fact, we still used them, but we found that certain modifications within the trials could make a huge difference. The discrete trials by themselves, without the motivational modifications, led to many problems. We were simply noticing that so many of the children we worked with weren't learning to talk, even after years of discrete trials targeting individual behaviors.

In that first study, our intervention focused on teaching first words to nonverbal children who hadn't been making progress using traditional procedures. Unfortunately, that was too often the case in the days of traditional discrete trial programs—about half the children never learned to use any consistent functional words. We chose verbal communication because it had been repeatedly documented as being particularly difficult to teach, requiring tens of thousands of trials of difficult and tedious shaping procedures to teach even a single word (cf. Lovaas, 1977). Although some children did learn words that way, teaching the thousands of words they would need to get by in everyday life was just too time consuming. To make matters worse, the shaping procedures weren't easy and required very skilled therapists (see Lovaas, 1977; Lovaas et al., 1973). Very few people were able to implement the approach successfully, and even fewer felt the approach was worth the massive amount of time required to produce the relatively limited improvements (see R.L. Koegel & Traphagen, 1982). That's why we were putting so much effort into figuring out better ways to speed up the process and improve the success rate.

> Determining the child's interests and involving parents in a nonclinical setting increased everyone's response and engagement.

Now on to the modifications. And to the successes. Our first study (R.L. Koegel et al., 1987) was successful beyond our wildest dreams. The children—many of whom had been nonverbal for the first 4, 5, or 6 years of their lives—were beginning to learn words. They were learning lots of words, and they were learning them quickly. These motivational components clearly were making a dramatic improvement when compared to a traditional discrete trial approach without the motivational components. The children began to acquire speech rapidly, sometimes even learning multiple words on the first day of intervention. Not only did the children's expressive verbal communication improve, but the children also produced words and word combinations spontaneously, and they generalized their newly acquired expressive communication to other environments—something that hadn't happened in the past.

One of the best things about the approach was that it was easy to implement—much easier than the discrete-trial shaping procedures. And it was a lot of fun, too. In fact, when we integrated a package of motivational variables into the teaching, it looked so easy and natural that we first called it the "Natural Language Paradigm." Ultimately, because the intervention positively affected many areas beyond speech and language, we renamed the approach "Pivotal Response Treatment." We've already mentioned the widespread improvement in positive behaviors, but perhaps equally important is the fact that later research (e.g., R.L. Koegel, Koegel, & Surratt, 1992) showed that when we were incorporating the motivational procedures, the children decreased or eliminated entirely their disruptive behavior without any

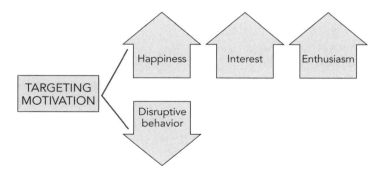

Changes associated with targeting motivation.

specific intervention aimed at that behavior. We didn't have to drag them into the sessions screaming and crying and gripping the doorjambs. They didn't hide when they saw the therapists driving up. They loved the sessions. Not only were they learning to talk at an incredibly rapid rate, but they were also enjoying the sessions, exhibiting almost no escape or avoidance behavior. And that's what it's all about. Later research (e.g., R.L. Koegel, Bimbela, & Schreibman, 1996; Schreibman, Kaneko, & Koegel, 1991; Vismara & Lyons, 2007) also showed that in addition to decreases in disruptive behavior there were improvements in the children's happiness, enthusiasm, and interest—*while* we were teaching them. It wasn't just the kids who improved, either. The children's parents were happier, more enthusiastic, and interested, too. They smiled more, taught more, and generally felt a lot better.

> Motivation is so core to everything that understanding it is essential to understanding autism. It may be that autism by itself, in early infancy, is a relatively minor problem. However, once a lack of motivation sets in, the children may fail to engage in every area that is necessary for typical development, and the problem becomes pervasive.

These findings were important for many reasons. First, we didn't need to punish the children to get them to respond—such nonaversive interventions are imperative for humanitarian reasons. Further, they are practical: If people enjoy what they're doing, they are likely to do more of it. Because improving the symptoms of autism requires a *lot* of intervention, it is especially important that the intervention be manageable and comfortable to implement—and punishment is neither. Next, when an intervention like this one can be comfortably woven into everyday lifestyles and routines, it is possible to provide a very intensive intervention without undue stress, and when intervention is pleasant, it is more likely that individuals with autism will engage in the newly learned behaviors outside of the teaching settings. Thus, an intervention can be implemented with less disruptive behavior and higher affect *and* it is likely to be used throughout the children's waking hours—all at a greatly reduced financial and emotional cost.

In short, motivation has proven to be a particularly pivotal area. As you'll see, it also underlies other pivotal areas, such as imitation and social behaviors. Motivation is not the only pivotal area, however. Next, we discuss another pivotal area that is critical for development.

Social Initiations and Question Asking

It is clear that certain behaviors lead to reciprocal responses from others in a child's environment and that those reciprocal interactions lead to important development. It's a cycle. For example, an early developing structure in typical language development is a simplified form of the question "What is that?" A typically developing child's first group of words usually includes a question along the lines of "Dat?" When a child says "Dat?"—usually while pointing to something—adults label objects. It's social, and it's educational. When a child asks "Dat?" repeatedly, it leads to huge gains in vocabulary. Wetherby and Prutting (1984) showed that children with autism typically do not ask questions. It's hard to believe, because they certainly must hear adults asking them "What's that?" all the time, but they don't. So we began researching ways to teach them to ask questions. L.K. Koegel, Camarata, Valdez-Menchaca, and Koegel (1998) showed that children with autism could easily be taught to ask "What is it?" When they did learn to ask the question, their vocabularies increased dramatically, without the vocabulary words even being taught. Thus, when the children asked the question, it led to subsequent teaching interactions from others in the children's natural environments—which is the way typically developing children learn and is much easier than teaching all the vocabulary words individually. Such self-initiations, where the child, without prompting, creates a learning opportunity through a social interaction, appeared to be a pivotal behavior, in that they resulted in widespread acquisition of other untreated behaviors. We also saw similar positive effects when we used question asking to target verbs (L.K. Koegel, Carter, & Koegel, 2003). Children with autism could easily learn to ask the question "What's happening?" or "What happened?" during or following an action, and when they asked one of these questions, the variety of verbs used and the correctness of their grammatical endings improved, without any specific intervention focused on teaching the verbs. Again, the children's pivotal behavior of question asking resulted in widespread gains.

These results got us thinking that we could probably target just about any language structure or morpheme by using questions. Along that line, we showed that children with autism could easily learn to ask "Where is it?" questions (e.g., "Where is the Gummi Bear?"), and when they asked such questions, the children rapidly acquired prepositions (e.g., the Gummi Bear is *under* the cup) (L.K. Koegel, Koegel, Green-Hopkins, & Barnes, 2010). Again, this learning happened without any direct intervention for teaching prepositions per se. The question asking was pivotal for acquiring many other behaviors.

> The more children are taught to actively find out about their environment, the more they learn, and the better they do in the long run.

And there's more. If you think about it, social initiations, such as questions, are the opposite of the withdrawal associated with autism. Using initiations should set up a series of transactional interactions that could result in very large gains in many areas. We showed that this was in fact the case (L.K. Koegel, Koegel, Shoshan, & McNerney, 1999). That is, with a comprehensive application of PRT, we found that when self-initiations (e.g., questions) occurred frequently, children with autism had especially favorable long-term treatment outcomes, sometimes being indistinguishable from typically developing children. The presence of this one behavior made a huge difference in the kids' lives. In the first phase of that study, we showed that preschool children who had initiations during naturalistic observational assessments ended up doing much better as adolescents or young adults than children who did not initiate interactions. In the second phase of the study, we showed that children who did not initiate could be taught a variety of initiations and that they subsequently had extremely favorable long-term treatment outcomes, again sometimes being almost or fully indistinguishable from typically developing children. These gains continued through adulthood.

Thus, it appears that motivation, self-initiations, and question asking are extremely important pivotal areas. The next section provides more evidence for why they make such a difference.

Robust Evidence for the Effectiveness of Focusing on Pivotal Skills

The scientific literature solidly shows that acquisition of pivotal skills is essential for accelerating the learning curve for children with autism. It is important to note that many studies have been conducted with a variety of different experimental designs, ranging from rigorous single-case designs to group statistical designs with random assignment to qualitative designs to clinical replication designs. That's a lot of technical words, and what it all means is that many different professionals have tested PRT with thousands of

This picture demonstrates how an adult can take advantage
of motivational activities to teach first words to a young child.

children in a variety of settings. It's important to know this
because there are so many interventions out there that are
purported to work but just don't. Because the critical period
of a child's life passes so quickly, there's no time to waste.
That's why good experimental designs are vitally important.

The experiments on PRT have been conducted in our
laboratories, clinics, and schools; with independent researchers collaborating with us; and in completely independent laboratories, clinics, and schools (the table in the
Introduction lists some of the main studies). In all cases,
when the children acquire pivotal skills, their functioning
improves. However, occasionally there are children who
just don't improve the way we would like. Although there
can be a tendency to describe these children who don't respond to intervention as "failures," we prefer to conceptu-

alize the "nonresponders" as needing a different teaching method. In other words, it's an issue for the teachers—not the students. In many cases, subsequent research on children who are not responding rapidly to PRT has shown that the method can be modified prescriptively so that a critical skill can be taught successfully to children who previously did not respond to the intervention.

For example, we recently showed that children who did not acquire speech with a usual PRT intervention learned to respond when we focused on attention to relevant cues while using the motivational components (R.L. Koegel, Shirotova, & Koegel, 2009a, 2009b). That is, once we got the children's attention on relevant cues, they showed the typical patterns of motivated responding and rapidly acquired words and then language, and, in most cases, made huge improvements. The results were dramatic, which emphasizes the importance of science in identifying new variables that need to be addressed during intervention. It's a constantly evolving process. It is also interesting that motivation played a critical role in establishing the children's attention to relevant cues. Thus, once again, motivation is central. Further support for the importance of motivation in the development of critical attention skills was shown in a study by Vismara and Lyons (2007). They found that when motivation was high, joint attention emerged in children with autism without any specific teaching; that is, children began looking back and forth between the communication partner and objects. The same finding was also reported by Bruinsma (2004). In this study, Bruinsma began implementing PRT with children who had no joint attention. About two months after the PRT started, joint attention emerged spontaneously. In Vismara and Lyon's study, as in Bruinsma's, joint attention typically emerged after about two months of PRT intervention (again without specific teaching) but could emerge almost instantly when the tasks involved materials and activities related to the child's intense interests. These types of "freebies" are really important, because the goal is to speed up the whole habilitation process.

Two important and practical questions, especially given the large numbers of children with autism, are who can teach PRT and in what types of settings it can be used. That is, can the procedures be implemented on a large enough scale to be meaningful for the millions of people in the world who could benefit from such an approach? As of this writing, two large-scale projects have been published showing that wide application of PRT is feasible and effective. Baker-Ericzén, Stahmer, and Burns (2007) showed that a community-based clinic could effectively deliver PRT to hundreds of children, with the children showing large improvement in adaptive behavior scale scores regardless of gender, age, or race or ethnicity. In another large-scale study, Bryson et al. (2007) and Smith et al. (2010) showed that it was feasible to implement PRT throughout the entire province of Nova Scotia, Canada. The data showed that, once trained, treatment providers throughout Nova Scotia could teach parents and other interventionists in a "trainer-of-trainers" model with fidelity of implementation over time. Most important, the children in the study, some of whom had little access to effective services prior to the study, made substantial progress on their targeted behaviors. Furthermore, this study also showed that a trainer-of-trainers model was effective in delivering PRT to many, many children who lived in very remote areas of the province and who did not have access to specialized clinics and centers.

In summary, the treatment of pivotal behaviors appears to be both feasible and important. Treatment providers and parents can easily learn how to target key pivotal areas such as motivation and self-initiated responding. Further, when they do so, very widespread improvements occur in children with autism, resulting in extremely positive long-term outcomes.

*M**yth:*** Every behavior your child lacks will need to be taught individually.

*R**eality:*** Focusing on pivotal areas will help your child progress faster.

*R**eality:*** Motivation may be the most important of the pivotal areas.

*R**eality:*** Personalizing the intervention for use with each child increases his or her engagement—and success.

*M**yth:*** Forcing children with autism to engage in difficult tasks will eventually improve their motivation.

*R**eality:*** Reinforcing the children for trying hard on difficult tasks will help their motivation.

MAKING IT WORK IN EVERYDAY SETTINGS: GETTING STARTED

As noted previously, it can take 10–20 years for a research finding to reach everyday life. What this means is that most of the interventions used in the real world are wildly outdated. Many children with autism are getting treatments that were developed literally decades ago. Although they work, they work slowly. That's why it is so important to use the newest interventions. However, it seems like new interventions are popping up each day, and you just don't have a lot of time to waste trying all of them.

If you're just getting started with PRT, there are a few important things you need to do to make sure that the PRT intervention is most effective in everyday settings:

■ *Look for data.* First, you need to be sure that the methods your interventionist is using are based on good scientific evidence. You need to investigate whether studies that support the treatment have been published in peer-reviewed journals. *Peer review* means that other scientists have checked whether the study has a good research design. This is so important.

■ *Find skilled people.* Once you have determined that the intervention is evidence-based, you need to make sure that your clinician is skilled in applying the intervention. Certification in PRT is available, and it must be renewed each year to ensure that the interventionist is using the procedures properly. Candidates must send video recordings of themselves working with children, so certification isn't just a matter of understanding the underlying concepts: Candidates actually have to *show* that they meet fidelity of implementation criteria, meaning that they meet a standardized and researched set of benchmarks.

■ *Define your targets and measure baselines.* Although research studies are one factor, you still need to make sure that you, the parent or the teacher, record data for the child with whom you are working. This means defining target behaviors clearly and specifically. This *doesn't* mean making vague statement such as, "We're working on her relationships with other people." The target needs to be specific, such as evaluating the number of minutes the child plays with a peer, the exact number of verbal reciprocal interactions she has with a peer (in addition to evaluating the quality of those interactions), what her play behavior is like with peers, how conflicts are resolved, and so forth. If you don't define a target and don't have baseline measurements, you will never be able to be sure that the child is improving. And some very good interventions don't work with some children, so it is important that you make ongoing measurements to be sure that your child is improving.

- *Provide a consistent approach.* Please don't be fooled by people who say they use an "eclectic" approach. Often this means that they know a little about a lot of things— not a lot about what works best. Further, research shows that an eclectic approach is less effective (Howard, Sparkman, Cohen, Green, & Stanislaw, 2004), so make sure your interventionist is delivering a consistent and comprehensive approach.

- *Stay updated.* You'll also want to make sure that you keep up with research findings, whether by reading journal articles, checking on our web sites (www.education.ucsb.edu/autism and www.koegelautism.com), or attending conferences. Major research centers publish their work on a regular basis, and you'll want to keep up with the latest and greatest findings.

- *Think big.* If a target behavior really isn't going to make a difference in the child's life, you may want to forget about it. Professionals call this "social significance." For example, if he knows how to go to the store and purchase items, it may not make a difference whether he can add fractions on a worksheet. If he can write a letter to a friend or relative, it may not matter whether he can complete those penmanship exercises perfectly. Every time you decide to work on a target behavior, you need to think, "Will this make a difference in this child's life?" If an interventionist can successfully teach a child to say "dog" but the child can't correctly identify the family pet, then this is not a significant gain. If an interventionist is trying to teach a young adult to decrease self-stimulatory behaviors, reducing the behavior by half (e.g., from 40% to 20%) is still not low enough for an adult to do well in a job interview or fit into social situations. Make sure that the target behavior will make a significant difference.

The bottom line is that the child needs to learn quickly, and the target behaviors need to produce positive changes in many other untargeted behaviors.

Ask Yourself

PARENTS & TEACHERS

1. Are the target behaviors I'm trying to teach going to lead to positive changes in other behaviors?
2. Are the target behaviors I'm trying to teach meaningful in the child's everyday life?
3. Am I focusing on pivotal areas, rather than just working on individual behaviors, so that the outcomes are more like those of a typically developing child, as opposed to nongeneralized, robotic-looking behavior changes?

How to Teach the Pivotal Area of Motivation

Travis is a teenager who was diagnosed with autism when he was a preschooler. Right before recess or lunch break he'll do anything—read, write, do math problems—but the rest of the day it's almost impossible to get him to finish his worksheets, complete his math, or write in his journal. Most of his life he's had a combination of general and special education, but now the school wants to decrease the amount of time that he's in a general education classroom, because they feel that he just isn't keeping up. The school called us to observe him and consult, because the family feels that he shouldn't be spending more time away from his typically developing peers.

This situation is not unusual. Kids on the spectrum don't always engage nicely in schoolwork like their typically developing peers. Often students with autism will engage in so much disruptive behavior that the teachers end up presenting really easy assignments. So although the child may be sitting quietly and completing assignments, he isn't learning anything at all. In the old days, most interventionists used to spend a lot of time trying to find rewards for on-task behavior and even punishing the children if they engaged in off-task or disruptive behaviors during academic tasks. That's really how we got into the whole area of motivation. We were working so hard, trying our darnedest to get them to learn how to talk, and to teach them to do math, to read, and to write. We tried everything, but it was rough. In fact, one time during a clinic session Bob jokingly said, "About the only thing they seem motivated to do is to get *out* of the session." We all chuckled a bit, but then we started thinking, Yes, they are pretty clever at figuring out unique ways to disrupt the sessions. And even though everyone says they are not social, in fact they are *so* socially astute that they notice the one instant the adult looks away and, in that instant, grab and devour the candies that are being used as rewards. To notice with that much subtlety is very socially aware! We also started realizing that some of the nonverbal kids, on rare occasion, said a word spontaneously. For example, now and again a child would say "Bye-bye!" Usually that was because the child didn't like the session, and, because we had lots of individual target behaviors to work on, we never let them go and just kept working. That was a big mistake. It's obvious now: If they talked and what they said didn't get rewarded, they learned that their behavior and the consequences that followed were unrelated. That caused a lack of trying. This got us thinking of the notion of learned helplessness.

LEARNED HELPLESSNESS

We hate to bring up the early studies on learned helplessness, because they are not pleasant, and we, personally, could have never run such studies, but they do give us interesting insights on behavior. Here goes. A long time ago, a group of researchers led by Martin Seligman did some studies that ended up revealing a phenomenon called learned helplessness (Seligman, Klein, & Miller, 1976; Seligman & Maier, 1967; Seligman, Maier, & Geer, 1968). The general paradigm for that research was to harness dogs on top of a pad that gave them electric shocks. At first the dogs tried desperately to get away, but because they were harnessed, they couldn't escape the shocks. Eventually, they stopped trying to get away. Although that makes sense, the most fascinating part is what happened next. The researchers took the harnesses off the dogs, and what do you think they did? If you guessed that they ran away, you're wrong. Believe it or not, they stood there and continued to let themselves get shocked. Yes, that's what they did. They didn't try to get away. They just simply stood there on the shock pad and endured the pain. In fact, the researchers tried lifting them off of the shock pad so they would know that they weren't harnessed, but when the researchers put them back on again, they still didn't try to get away. You're probably thinking, "What the heck was wrong with those dogs?" Right? Well, eventually the researchers decided that instead of picking the dogs up off the shock pad, they would nudge them off, giving them a simple little nudge so that the dogs would get off the pad on their own. Well, that did it. Once the dogs were prompted to get off, *on their own*, they became motivated to escape, and from then on, they ran off the shock pad. Well, the moral of the story, from a conceptual point of view, was this: If the dogs understood that their response (jumping off the shock pad) was related to the consequence (escaping the shock), they continued to try to get off.

Although we don't know whether an exact parallel can be made between animal studies and humans, we do know that a similar phenomenon seems to occur with people. That is, if consequences are not contingent, the person stops trying. This effect can happen with both noncontingent punishment and noncontingent rewards. Think about kids who grow up in very wealthy families and get everything they want. If the things they want are given to them contingently, they are likely to become successful adults. However, if the things are given to them noncontingently, they are likely to become lazy and unproductive adults. It's all a matter of a child learning how his or her behavior affects the surround-

| Adult puts on the jacket for the child. | Child does not help put on the jacket. | Adult continues to put on the entire jacket. | Adult stops putting on the jacket for the child. | Child does not try to put on the jacket on his or her own. |

Process of learned helplessness.

| Adult guides the child to put on the jacket. | Child finishes the final step of the jacket. | Adult starts to fade assistance with the jacket. | Adult stops putting on the jacket for the child. | Child tries to put on the jacket on his or her own. |

Successful treatment of learned helplessness.

ing world, and if positive or negative consequences are de-livered noncontingently, there's going to be a problem.

Now, let's talk about what can happen with children with autism. No one will disagree that lots of things are difficult for these children. Talking is difficult; social interaction is dif-ficult; even everyday tasks can be difficult. If well-meaning adults "help" the children too much, so that the children do not have to try, they are likely to stop trying. We've seen chil-dren who spent most of their day "spaced out," with adults physically motoring them through every activity. If someone always dressed a child because he dressed himself too slowly, the child was likely to just stand there and let everyone con-tinue to dress him. Likewise, if a child never has to talk for anything and gets everything she needs while remaining silent, she probably won't start talking.

So instead of creating learned helplessness, the idea is to get the kids responding—to get them *motivated*. There are very specific ways to get a child motivated, that is, to get them responding more often, more rapidly, and with more enthusiasm. This chapter reviews these motivational procedures one by one and then shows how to put them together as a group so that they are especially potent.

MOTIVATION: IMPORTANT POINTS

Child Choice

Loads of studies have shown that kids on the spectrum do much better with a task if they are allowed some choice in

Comparison of discrete trial training and Pivotal Response Treatment (PRT)

	Discrete trial format	PRT
Stimulus items	Chosen by clinician Repeated until criterion is met	Chosen by child Varied every few trials Combination of maintenance and acquisition tasks
Interaction	Clinician holds up stimulus item Stimulus item is not functionally related to interaction	Clinician and child play with stimulus item Stimulus item is used functionally within the interaction
Environment	Teaching procedures take place in a structured setting	Teaching procedures take place in the context of naturally occurring activities
Response	Only correct responses are reinforced	Reasonable attempts that are clear and goal oriented are reinforced
Reinforcement	Arbitrary reinforcers (typically edibles) are provided immediately after the child's response	Natural reinforcers are provided immediately after response

the activity. We prefer that the choice be related to the task materials, so that a child gets a natural reinforcer tied into his or her response. For example, if a child who is learning to say her first words wants a toy, having her verbally request the toy is a perfect example of child choice, because the toy can be given to her as a reward. Although this seems perfectly logical, and you may be saying to yourself, "Yeah! That's a no-brainer," there are several instances in which choice could be used but is not. For example, many professionals use flashcards for teaching. There are thousands of ready-made flashcard kits for just about any purpose—learning verbs, saying articulation sounds,

Child Choice

Use child-preferred or child-selected materials, topics, and toys, and follow the child's lead during interactions.

learning "he" versus "she." You name it, and you can find a flashcard for it. For the most part, though, kids on the spectrum don't have a say in selecting these types of teaching materials. Instead of this, in our work we like to use items that would be found in the child's natural environment and let her choose from those items. Further, most kids prefer those exciting toys and activities rather than sitting at a table and using flashcards. On many, many occasions we've seen a child happily playing with an appropriate toy—a perfect stimulus for a learning opportunity—but then a parent or another well-meaning adult says, "Look at this cool toy," and directs the child to another toy or directs her back to the table to work with flashcards. Although the other toy may have been cool or the flashcards might have made the therapist's job easier, they weren't what the child was initially interested in. Thus, the parent or therapist has just changed the activity from a child-choice activity to an adult-choice activity—*even if* the child appears to become interested in the new activity. Well, most people who spend time around

This child actively engages in social and learning interactions when favorite activities are incorporated into the treatment.

kids have been guilty of this one, and with typically developing kids it may not matter, because they're often interested in just about anything, but with kids on the spectrum it's really important to follow their lead and give them choice.

This next example may be unbelievable, but sadly it's true. We were asked to consult in a school that claimed to be using PRT. The school administration had us take a look at a young boy who was fully included into a general kindergarten classroom. When we entered the classroom, this child was running wildly around the room, not engaging in any activities, with the classroom aide close on his heels. We watched for about 15 minutes while this activity (or lack of it) continued. Finally, we asked the staff if they were doing PRT with him. They responded that of course they were. When we queried as to what PRT point they were implementing, they responded with "child choice," saying that his choice was to run around the classroom, so they were letting him. Of course, we immediately escorted him over to a table and asked him what (appropriate) activity he wanted to engage in. We then explained to the staff that child choice, or following the child's lead, means having specific target behaviors and using child-preferred activities or stimulus items during teaching opportunities. Running around the classroom and doing nothing *isn't* a teaching opportunity.

Next, we should mention that some activities seem to allow little, if any, choice. However, this is not true. It's just that a little imagination is required. For example, kids have to do homework, and homework isn't always fun. Although it may seem hard to see opportunities for choice under these circumstances, they're there. You can always give the child the choice of the order in which the assignments are done or offer to let him go in any room to complete his homework. You can offer him the choice of what color pencil or pen he wants to use. Be creative. Offer choices even when there don't seem to be any. It will make a big difference.

One last word: Kids like choice so much that we've even seen it work with disruptive behaviors. For example, a little preschooler we were working with didn't want to leave the session to go home, so he lay down on the floor and began to have a tantrum. After a few minutes, when we could see it wasn't going to end soon, we asked him if he wanted to walk to the car or be carried. He immediately got up and said, "Walk!" Choice works, even when it's between two undesired things!

Interspersal of Acquisition and Maintenance Tasks

Much of Lynn's original training as a speech-language pathologist and educational psychologist involved figuring out what a child's deficits were and then developing practice exercises to target those behaviors. It worked well with children who had mild disabilities, but the kids with autism generally became disruptive during the sessions. To understand the reason why, recall the idea of learned helplessness. Children with autism have so many areas of need; consequently, they experience failure constantly. The reaction of giving up—learned helplessness—becomes very easy. Thus, if the practice exercises are so challenging that we repeatedly present difficult "acquisition" tasks, children with autism may find them just too demanding and give up on trying the task. They instead become disruptive in order to escape the task. However, we learned that if we interspersed acquisition tasks with tasks that the children had already mastered, they did a lot better.

Interspersal of Maintenance and Acquisition Tasks

Intersperse numerous, previously learned tasks with occasional new skills the child has not already learned.

One of our daughters, who is currently pursuing her Ph.D. in special education, makes the following analogy to sports. She says that coaches always work kids up gradually so that they experience success. They don't start with hardball or fast-pitch softball; they start with T-ball. You get the idea. If someone experiences success, he or she is likely to try harder. If the person constantly experiences failure, he or she is likely to give up. Interspersing tasks the children have already mastered amid new tasks helps their motivation. You might think that all those trials of easy tasks slow the learning down, but they don't. The children actually learn faster when acquisition and maintenance tasks are interspersed. Some people have described the underlying theory as "behavioral momentum," which basically means that if you do a bunch of things right—one after another—you get this "momentum" that helps carry you through the harder activity. It may lessen your frustration or just get you motivated to respond harder (or respond at all) on those more difficult tasks. We all can relate to that. With kids on the spectrum, it seems even more significant that they experience success. Thus, for learning new tasks, it is important that previous successes be mixed together with the harder tasks.

Task Variation

Task variation is a close cousin to interspersal of acquisition and maintenance tasks. The short of it is *don't* drill, drill, drill. Please! Everyone remembers those pages and pages of math homework that were difficult and repetitious. In fact, we struck a deal with one of our daughter's teachers about these pesky math problems. We would cut the number of homework problems way down, because there were just far too many and she was making mistakes—not because she couldn't do the problems but because of fatigue. On the other hand, she would be graded on the smaller number of problems, so each problem carried more weight. The shorter number of problems allowed her to switch tasks more frequently, rather than having to work for a long period of time on just the math task. This deal worked fabulously, and we should mention that she finished all her course work in medical school, so skipping a few math problems in elementary school didn't seem to hurt! Anyway, the idea here is to vary the tasks and not present any one task for a long period of time without anything else interspersed. Kids do better when the tasks are shorter and mixed up. Don't stay with one target behavior too long, even if the child is doing well. Keep varying the tasks and keep the child interested.

> *Task Variation*
>
> Vary the stimulus items and reinforcers during interactions.

Natural Reinforcement

It wasn't that long ago that, for the both of us, conducting a treatment session meant gathering stacks of flashcards, practicing the tasks on the flashcards with the child, and giving the child small treats for responding well. In fact, we even did research on the rewards, such as whether varying the treats improved the child's responding. We never really gave much thought to the notion of natural reinforcers. In fact, when the child asked nicely to leave, we didn't let him go if we were in the middle of a session. Things sure have changed since then. With the use of natural reinforcers, the children are much more motivated, engaged, and responsive. For example, we remember working with a 5-year-old boy who had never said a word. He imitated a few sounds on request but never really said a word per se. One day he really wanted one of the cookies we had brought for a reward for some nonverbal task we were working on, and we just decided to use the cookie to work on expressive words. We held up the cookie and said, "Cookie," which of course he had heard many times. We paused and modeled the word a few more times. "Each time we did this, to our delight, he carefully but accurately pronounced "Coo-kie!" and of course each time he got a generous bite of the cookie. Before that time, he had never, ever, said a word. You can see, in this simple example, that using the desired cookie for a natural reinforcer, rather than a reinforcer for a totally unrelated activity, made an enormous difference in his progress.

From then on, natural reinforcers have been a regular part of our program. Regardless of the activity, if natural rewards are used, you'll see a big difference in the child's

> ### *Natural Reinforcers*
> Use reinforcers that are directly and functionally related to the task.

responsiveness. For example, if you're teaching a child to dress independently, you may want to have him put on his jacket in a chilly room rather than a hot room. If you're teaching a child to tie her shoes, have her do it just before going outside. No matter what the activity, there is almost always an opportunity to use a natural reward, if you give it some thought. Even advanced activities, such as fractions, can be practiced with delicious recipes. During writing activities, children can write sentences about what they want to do (and of course you'll let them do it right after the sentence), instead of a teacher-selected topic. With a bit of creativity, most activities can be tied into natural reinforcers, and you'll have a much happier, social, and involved learner, with less disruptive behavior, if the behavior has a natural reward.

Reinforcing Attempts

We were in a session once in which the dad repeatedly said "No" to the child even though the boy was trying as hard as he could to do the task. Of course, we gave him feedback, suggesting that, rather than punishing his child, he could reward the child's attempts by saying "Good try. Try again." Rewarding attempts is particularly important for children with autism, who have, indeed, experienced repeated failures. Regardless of whether they perform correctly or not, they need to be rewarded for trying. Now, don't get this confused with responding when the child didn't try. Sometimes kids will give a half-hearted attempt that happens to be correct or will respond while looking inattentively around the room. Do not reward these types of responses. They are not

> ### *Reinforcing Attempts*
> Reinforce reasonable attempts that are clear, unambiguous, and goal oriented.

attempts. Attempts must be free of inappropriate behaviors, and it must be clear that the child is *really* trying. In those situations the child should be rewarded, even if he isn't 100% correct. The child's motivation will improve significantly if each and every true attempt, no matter how close it is to the end desired behavior, is rewarded.

SCIENTIFIC EVIDENCE FOR MOTIVATION AS A PIVOTAL AREA

Not only did our initial research show that motivation was hugely effective with communication, but later research showed that motivation is also immensely important in the teaching of so many other areas for individuals with autism. It is important to understand that each of the procedures that make up the PRT approach to motivation has been carefully studied.

To start with, in 1979 we (R.L. Koegel & Egel) speculated that children with autism had a "learned helplessness." Recall those early studies by Seligman et al. (1967, 1968, 1976): If consequences (either rewards or punishers) are not connected to a behavior, the result is a lack of trying. We thought that this might be the reason children with autism often don't try to learn new tasks. It appears as if the children think they can't do things that they actually are capable of doing. We discussed this idea in an article entitled "Motivation in Childhood Autism: Can They or Won't They?" (R.L. Koegel & Mentis, 1985). In this article we speculated that the children's learned helplessness causes them to attempt to escape or avoid what they think might be difficult social interactions. Furthermore, they avoid learning situations because they erroneously feel that they can't be successful in them. We hypothesized that this avoidance and escape from social interactions and other learning opportunities then resulted in the children's failing to learn important skills necessary for development and, in turn, resulted in the eventual full-blown disorder of autism. It's just one big vicious cycle. To solve this problem, we hypothesized that if the children could learn that their behavior was related to the consequences of their behavior, then the severity of the autism might be reversed and the children would rapidly improve. That is, if intervention focused on increasing their motivation to engage in social communication as well as increasing their motivation to try to learn other tasks, the result was likely to be a major improvement in the children's overall development. Again, finding the key underlying problem—which we hypothesized was a lack of motivation—would make the big difference.

This focus on decreasing learned helplessness was hugely successful in identifying numerous powerful motivational variables that, individually, were extremely effective in increasing the motivation of children with autism to engage in social interactions and make academic and other learning gains. These days, the motivational aspect of PRT is viewed as a "package" that encompasses five strategies: child choice of stimulus materials, use of natural reinforcers, reinforcement for attempts, interspersal of maintenance and acquisition tasks, and variation of tasks. The empirical evidence for each of these individual component variables is described separately below, as is the evidence for the dramatic effectiveness of the combined package.

Choice of Stimulus Materials

One of the first motivational variables we discovered was child choice. It sounds illogical now, but when we used the discrete trial format, the clinicians pretty much chose all of the stimulus materials—which largely consisted of flashcards. Yes. Boring flashcards. However, when the children could choose the stimulus materials to be used in the learning interactions, their motivation was dramatically higher. The effectiveness of choice has been so powerful that tons of studies now document this fact—for all kinds of people (Kern et al., 1998; R.L. Koegel, Dyer, & Bell, 1987).

In the area of autism, we even did some research on conversation and choice (R.L. Koegel, Dyer, et al., 1987). We showed that when children with autism were able to choose the topic of discussion or the type of play they could engage in during a social interaction, their motivation improved, and they became more social. Also, the data showed that if we taught the children to steer the interaction toward their preferred area of interest, their social interactions also improved. Now, this doesn't mean that everyone has to spend the rest of their lives interacting with the children about their restricted interests; it's just a great way to get them to be more social during the beginning stages of their learning. As the children become more motivated and better conversationalists, parents, teachers, and therapists can start teaching them how to be good listeners, to ask questions, and to respond empathetically. But, remember, the first step is always to get them motivated.

Natural Reinforcers

A second finding that had a large impact on improving children's motivation to learn involved the response–reinforcer connection itself. We speculated that natural reinforcers—or, to put it simply, rewards that were directly related to the behavior we were teaching—would produce faster and more generalized learning (Skinner, 1954, 1986). That is, when a target response was directly (rather than indirectly) related to the reinforcer, children might learn more rapidly with more generalized gains. For example, if we were teaching a child to open a lunchbox, we placed a favorite food inside the lunchbox, rather than teaching the child to open the lunchbox and then handing her a treat (R.L. Koegel & Williams, 1980). What's also interesting is that when the response–reinforcer relationship is natural, meaningful, and direct, then affect improves as well, suggesting that the children are more interested in learning (R.L. Koegel & Williams, 1980; Williams, Koegel, & Egel, 1981). Dunlap and Kern (1996) and Hinton and Kern (1999) also confirmed this finding with children who had other severe disabilities. For example, a child who was failing to learn to write, and who exhibited severe disruptive behavior to avoid the writing task, showed greatly improved learning and affect when the writing tasks were made more meaningful (i.e., when they directly related to a natural reinforcer), such as writing a letter to a meaningful person.

Similarly, one could teach other concepts in a meaningful way by using a variety of materials (e.g., teaching time concepts by using a bus schedule). Kazdin (1977) speculated that a natural, direct response–reinforcer contingency might be more effective than an indirect reinforcer in part because the direct contingency and the target response occur in very close temporal and physical proximity to the reinforcer. For example, in the illustration mentioned above, when the children are learning how to open a lunchbox, the food inside the lunchbox provides a natural reinforcer delivered in close proximity to the response of opening the lid. In contrast, when the reinforcer is delivered in a way that is indirectly related to the response (as when the clinician hands a reinforcer to a child after she has tried to open the lunchbox), interfering behaviors (such as reaching for the reward) may occur between the target response and the delivery of the reinforcer. That sounds pretty complicated, but the interesting thing is that the child gets the same reward either way. So why would it make a difference? Well, to be meaningful within the interaction, there has to be a direct link between the reinforcer and the behavior.

In a related area of research, we wondered if the same positive effect could be achieved with social rewards. We (R.L. Koegel, Vernon, & Koegel, 2009) showed that if social interactions were embedded into the delivery of a natural reinforcer, the children became more social. For example, if we were teaching verbal communication, one way to provide a natural reward would be the following: When the child makes a verbal request to jump on a trampoline, we give the child an opportunity to jump on the trampoline as a natural reward. In such a case, the child's motivation to request would improve, but there would probably be very little improvement in social behavior. In contrast, if the adult joined the child on the trampoline after the child made the request, the child would become more social as well as more communicative. Again, this body of research demonstrates that including reinforcers that are intrinsically and directly tied to the desired target behaviors improves the children's motivation to attempt the tasks. This strategy works with communication, behavior, and even social engagement.

Reinforcing Attempts

One of the biggest and most surprising breakthroughs in the area of motivation and autism was the discovery that reinforcing children's attempts to learn a task—even if their responses were incorrect—was more effective than reinforcing them for making correct responses in a strict motor-shaping paradigm. Prior to that, most behaviors were taught by using a shaping paradigm. This approach was challenging for many clinicians because they could only reward the child's behaviors that were equal to or better than the previous response. That sounds easy, but when you're working on a behavior such as first words, it's sometimes challenging to be completely accurate. In addition, because so many of the target behaviors are really, really difficult for the children, often they didn't get all that many rewards. However, in contrast, and in direct support of the learned helplessness theory, the data showed that if attempts were rewarded the children began to exhibit many responses that had, to everyone's surprise, apparently been in their repertoires all along but just were not being used. Even if it was a completely new behavior, they at least tried a lot harder.

For example, one of the first studies we conducted in this area (R.L. Koegel, O'Dell, & Dunlap, 1988) was with nonverbal children with autism, who really hadn't learned any consistent words over a period of many years when we used a shaping intervention (wherein successively more correct responses were reinforced). In contrast to their previous failure to acquire speech, when their verbal attempts were rewarded, they rapidly acquired large vocabularies. The important idea here is "attempt." If they responded correctly but didn't seem to be trying, we didn't reward them—they really had to be trying. But if they did try—even if their attempt wasn't correct or wasn't as good or better that the previous response—we rewarded them. The speed with which the children began to produce words and word approximations when their attempts were rewarded was incredibly rapid. And this was after years of ineffective intervention with this subgroup of nonverbal children. That's why we titled the resulting article *"producing* speech use" in nonverbal children with autism rather than *"acquisition* of speech" in nonverbal children with autism. Because they were learning so quickly, it appeared that the children may have been capable of producing many words but were not attempting to produce them.

Although we hoped that the children might come out with an entire full vocabulary without any teaching, that was not the case. Instead, they still needed to learn the words, but they just learned them at an extremely rapid rate, more like how typically developing children acquire words.

In addition, following the intervention, the children (like typically developing children) began to pick up vocabulary words through observation of others in their environment, without needing direct intervention—another positive-collateral outcome.

With the discovery of these motivational variables, it began to look like the search for the pivotal behavior of imitation that began in the 1960s finally seemed to be successful. That is, it appeared that if the children became motivated enough, they would begin to imitate, and this in turn produced widespread, rapid learning. Thus, these studies again suggested that motivation was a core problem that needed to be addressed before the children would make important gains through other areas such as imitation.

Interspersal of Maintenance and Acquisition Tasks

Another component in the motivational package relates to interspersal of easy and difficult tasks. In an important study, Dunlap (1984) showed that part of the problem with motivation in children with autism was the way that interventionists approached teaching the target goals. That is, we always focused on teaching the children tasks that they didn't know how to do. Although this strategy appeared logical at first glance, we were working repetitively on new, difficult tasks and did not consider the fact that that could be very demanding and frustrating for the learner—especially a child with autism. For someone with learned helplessness, this approach could be a disaster. However, we found out that if we mixed the new tasks with tasks that the child already knew, the child was far more motivated to learn new and difficult tasks. We called this interspersal of acquisition and maintenance tasks. So great was the difference that even using a ratio of seven to one for maintenance to acquisition trials, the children made far greater gains than when we taught only acquisition tasks. In hindsight this makes sense. If people are motivated to learn, they will learn rapidly. If they are motivated to leave the teaching situation, they may learn very little, if anything, from the instruction. Thus, paradoxically, interspersing a large number of maintenance trials keeps the child engaged and excited even when the difficult new tasks come up every so often.

Carr, Newsom, and Binkoff (1976) reported a similar result when they showed that "burying" a demand within a string of easy requests results in the children complying with the demand, even with individuals who had previously tried to escape the demand by using extremely severe behaviors, such as self-injury. This same type of strategy has been effective with other populations. For example, Singer, Singer, and Horner (1987) showed that people with mental retardation would comply with a previously refused difficult demand if the demand was preceded by a string of easy demands. Some have discussed this phenomenon as behavioral momentum. Behavioral momentum means that the students pick up a momentum to respond, and because they have this momentum they continue to respond when the new, difficult demand is added to the string of easy tasks.

Task Variation

Closely related to the idea of interspersal is task variation. Specifically, we showed that when tasks are frequently varied, as opposed to presenting a single task repetitively in a drill-practice format, children are more motivated to learn, and they learn more quickly (Dunlap & Koegel, 1980). That is, correct responding, rate of responding, and positive affect improved. And that's the whole idea—for the kids to be learning quickly and having fun at the same time.

Again, in hindsight, this seems logical. For example, how many typically developing children ever learned a concept such as size by sitting down at a table and pointing repeatedly to the big versus the little object? Not many. Typically developing children are naturally exposed to interspersed trials related to size or other concepts. It probably shouldn't be surprising, then, that this also seems to be the best strategy for teaching children with autism. This strategy of providing trials interspersed naturally throughout the day seems to produce less frustration and avoidance than sitting down and intensively providing drill practice on the same task. Plus, it's a lot more fun for the adults too!

Overall Motivational Package

As these variables that are related to improving motivation and overall learning for children with autism were being discovered, two thoughts occurred to us. First, we were very excited that motivational variables were being discovered, when only a few years earlier it had seemed almost impossible to motivate children with autism to attempt difficult learning tasks (e.g., social communication). Now many different procedures were working. It was becoming easy to motivate the children to engage in social communication. This was exciting.

However, we began to wonder where all this was headed. Was there some connection among all of these variables? We wondered if it might be possible to combine all of them into a single package. It seemed that such a package might be extremely powerful. It could also be very difficult to implement. Surprisingly, however, when the variables were combined and implemented in unison, the combined package looked amazingly like natural interactions among typically developing children. Although this was a very systematic approach, it looked like the children were playing and having a great time, which made the intervention appealing to interventionists, teachers, clinicians, parents, and

Good and bad examples of Pivotal Response Treatment components

	Goal	Bad example	Good example
Child choice	Learn colors	Use arbitrary items to label colors, such as using construction paper to teach red and white.	Use the child's favorite toys or items to label colors, such as playing with a fire truck to teach red and white.
Interspersal of maintenance and acquisition tasks	Complete homework assignment	Only work on new subtraction problems.	Mix many simple tasks the child enjoys with occasional new subtraction problems.
Direct and natural reinforcers	Differentiate fast versus slow	Wave a pencil at different speeds in front of the child and have the child label each movement as fast or slow.	Play ball and have the child ask for a fast or a slow pitch; pitch the ball as requested.
	Initiate wh– questions	Child points to a bag and says "What's that?" and is given an M&M and told "Good question."	Child points to a bag and says "What's that?" and a desired item is then pulled out of the bag.
	Follow instructions	Child is shown a picture book and instructed to "Touch cup"; therapist says "Great job!" and turns the page if the child gives a correct response.	Child correctly responds to the instruction "Touch cup"; after the child finds the cup, the therapist hands the child the cup, which contains a small amount of juice.
Reinforce attempts	First words	Child says "ba" for ball and is instructed to say the whole word.	Child says "ba" for ball and is immediately given a ball.

others. Punishments weren't necessary, and the children learned quickly. Quite simply, we took a traditional, discrete trial approach and systematically included the variables of choice, natural reinforcers, interspersal, and task variation within the discrete trial paradigm. The results were dramatic. They produced generalized speech use in previously nonverbal children with autism (R.L. Koegel, O'Dell, et al., 1987). The rate of learning was dramatically faster than when a discrete trial approach was used without the specific motivational variables. Further, the children used their substantial amounts of speech in widely generalized contexts, suggesting that they not only had learned the words but also were motivated to use them in a variety of contexts. Perhaps most important, it was clear (from measured affect rating scales) that the children were greatly enjoying the sessions—they didn't try to escape, avoid, or become disruptive during the intervention. They smiled more, seemed more interested, were more engaged, and, consequently, learned faster. A further plus was that their parents' affect also improved while implementing the PRT package—they enjoyed it more, smiled more, had better interactions with their children, showed lower levels of stress, and provided more learning opportunities.

As you can see in the table in the Introduction, our center and others have tested the package of motivational variables. The results have consistently shown that the children are capable of far more than had previously been suspected. Once motivated, the children show significantly larger gains in speech, social behavior, academic success, joint attention, and symbolic play. Their levels of happiness, interest, and enthusiasm are all dramatically higher. In fact, instead of having negative affect, such as crying and tantrums, they have very positive affect, such as smiling, laughing, and even initiating additional interactions—which is precisely the point of the whole process.

Myth: Children with autism do best with repeated drill-practice trials on their deficits.

Reality: Incorporating motivational procedures into the intervention decreases disruptive behavior, improves interest and happiness, and speeds up learning.

MAKING IT WORK IN EVERYDAY SETTINGS

To make the motivational procedures work, you first need to create opportunities. Even with the motivational components, most kids on the spectrum won't initially beg for intervention. You won't see them initiating social interactions (see Chapter 4 on self-initiations) in the early stages, and they are likely to still try to do almost everything completely independently just to avoid social communication. So it is very important to create opportunities for communication or any other behavior that you would like to target. This means changing your mindset completely. You'll need to be proactive and think about every instance that motivates your child. If he likes to go on car rides, he'll need to say something about the ride each and every time. As his skills improve, you can add responses such as getting the keys out, buckling up, turning on the ignition, and going. We had one child who loved to go on car rides with his dad. They had a routine where they counted down from 10 before they took off: 10—9—8—and so forth until they got to 1—then the whole family exclaimed, "Blast off!" and the dad started driving. When the child was having some difficulty with multiplication, we decided to have the family incorporate that into the driving game. Instead of counting down from 10, they started multiplying 10 times 1, 10 times 2, etc.—10, 20, 30, 40, 50, 60—until they got to 100, then they "blasted off" (drove away). We had them replicate this with fives and then other numbers. In this way, boring multiplication tables that needed regular practice turned into a fun family game.

If you are a teacher, consider this unfortunate fact: In a school setting, most children with autism are provided with only about one opportunity an hour to use expressive communication. That isn't a typo—*once* an hour. If you are gasping, you are probably one of those teachers who is an exception to the rule, but the average teacher provides only one opportunity an hour throughout the entire day. Kids on the spectrum, who already have such a significant deficit in the area of communication, need to have consistent, frequent opportunities to use verbal communication, and you can start by setting up repeated opportunities in your classroom. If the child likes going outside to play, have her ask to go out, open the door, tell you what she will do outside, and so forth. Lunch and snack times usually provide perfect opportunities for the child to request foods, and for some children who are less interested in toys but love snacks, you can use each potato chip for an opportunity or cut the child's sandwich in small pieces to provide more opportunities. The goal is to have the children become good conversationalists at the lunch or dinner table, and this strategy makes a good start toward that end.

In the beginning, most of the opportunities you will create will be for the children to request items and activities they want. It's a simple but important starting point: They are learning that although talking is difficult, it leads to a desired outcome. Over time, once they become more enthusiastic about using communication, you can look for opportunities that are more social. The important thing to look for first is whether motivational components are a part of everyday interactions for your child. These variables can be incorporated in almost all activities, including schoolwork.

When you make sure there are natural reinforcers associated with the task, it is more likely to be meaningful. And as a teacher or parent, you'll be a lot happier when your child is an enthusiastic and interested learner. That will happen when you make sure that motivational components are incorporated into the teaching tasks.

Ask Yourself

PARENTS

1. Am I giving my child choices?
2. Am I interspersing easy and difficult tasks?
3. Am I reinforcing "trying"?
4. Are the activities I am providing for my child leading to a natural reinforcer?
5. Is my child provided with opportunities to use expressive communication throughout the day?

TEACHERS

1. Am I incorporating motivational activities into the curriculum?
2. Am I giving my student choices?
3. Am I reinforcing "trying"?
4. Am I interspersing easy and difficult tasks?
5. Is my student receiving natural reinforcers that are leading to meaningful outcomes?
6. Is my student getting opportunities throughout the day to use expressive verbal communication that has a meaningful outcome?

3

How to Get Rid of Disruptive Behavior

Not long ago, our team was meeting with a group of really wonderful and dedicated parents and professionals from all over the United States who were working with children, adolescents, and adults with autism. We were discussing different types of intervention, and one of the parents from the East Coast looked at us and said, "There's a perception around the country that you only work with high-functioning children and don't see disruptive children." That's verbatim. When we heard that, we almost fell off our chairs laughing. We asked the parent if people thought that all the children in the Santa Barbara area (and we work regularly and directly with most of the children with autism in this area) were born without disruptive behavior? She immediately joined in our laughter.

Although we joked about it, we had to agree with the workshop participant that the children we work with really don't have much disruptive behavior. It's not because they were born that way. It's because of the motivational procedures we use. The bottom line? If kids are having fun, they're not going to be disruptive.

Now then, you're probably wondering, why doesn't everyone use the motivational procedures? Here's why: training. It is a lot easier to train someone to hold up a preprinted flashcard and ask "What's that?" than it is to train someone to follow the child's lead, find something that interests that child, present the teaching opportunity interspersed within

This child is learning appropriate replacement behaviors so that he can have fun playing with his little brother rather than engaging in aggression or disruptive behavior.

maintenance, and then contingently provide a natural rein-forcer. It sounds easy and makes sense, but almost no one meets our fidelity of implementation requirements—even at the minimum 80% level—without a lot of feedback. And many of the people we train have master's and doctoral de-grees. It's much easier to just use a standard package with everyone, but that's not what's best for the child. However, when the motivational procedures are being implemented correctly, we see very little, if any, disruptive behavior.

That being said, most—and for some children *all*—disruptive behaviors are communicative. Because all indi-viduals with autism have difficulties with communication, there are going to be times when they are frustrated, bored, tired, hungry, or any of the other states of being that are challenging for all of us. However, when someone doesn't have the communication to express these feelings, they will be expressed through disruptive behavior, especially if the disruptive behavior works or has worked in the past. The answer to the treatment of disruptive behavior lies in understanding the motivation behind it. People are not disruptive because they are bad. They are disruptive because they (typically) are trying to avoid a task that's too difficult or because they are trying to get attention but just don't have the words. In fact, we've seen many school-aged children with autism who were trying to interact with peers, except they were using inappropriate behaviors.

TYPICAL DEVELOPMENT AND DISRUPTIVE BEHAVIOR

This phenomenon isn't unique to children with autism. Consider the behavior of typically developing children, who initially, as infants, communicate by crying. It is all they know how to do. Once they begin to learn to talk, crying decreases dramatically. However, young children will occasionally revert to the more primitive form of communicating by crying. Most parents will say something to the child such as "Use your words" or "Don't cry." With this type of prompting and follow-through, the children begin to use their more advanced form of communication: talking. Talking is a lot more socially acceptable in the real world than crying. And certain words are particularly useful. In Chapter 4, on self-initiations, we discuss teaching a child to initiate the word "Help" when a task is too difficult. Once children learn to use their words in meaningful ways, they find that words are extremely useful in getting the desired results and they usually don't revert to those early forms of communication, such as throwing tantrums. The problem is that children with autism have such difficulty learning to talk. That is why PRT is so valuable, because it motivates the children to try to talk and the ability to talk eliminates most disruptive behavior.

Now, let's consider the case of a child who seeks attention by being disruptive. Again, we need to look at the motivation to initiate. If the child is motivated, then it is easy to
teach the child social initiations to seek attention. The child
can be taught to initiate a word such as "Look!" to show her
parent what she has been doing. Other initiations are also
useful. For example, asking questions can not only gain attention but can also increase knowledge. Even the small percentage of children who are truly nonverbal can be taught to
use appropriate communication by means of a sign, picture
card, or computerized device. The response you're teaching
just has to have the same function as the problem behavior.

The important thing to remember is that when a child
is being disruptive, there is a reason for it. Often the reason relates to the child's learned helplessness. And often the
disruptive behavior has been effective, efficient, or even inadvertently rewarded by an adult. However, once the child
is empowered through motivation, disruptive behavior
becomes unnecessary. Many, many studies have been conducted on functional analysis, and the importance of understanding any problem behavior cannot be understated.
Children with autism exhibit disruptive behavior for escape
and avoidance functions. That is, they are trying to escape
or avoid difficult social communication tasks, difficult academic tasks, etc. With PRT, we are hypothesizing that if the
children are motivated to engage in social communication,
academic tasks, etc., then they will not exhibit disruptive behavior to escape or avoid the tasks. In contrast, they will be
motivated to perform appropriate behaviors so they will not
terminate the motivational activities. Thus for children with
autism, it is critical to consider the pivotal area of motivation,
which is central to eliminating disruptive behavior. People
are often surprised to see that disruptive behavior disap-
pears in children that are properly motivated to perform
appropriate behaviors. That benefit is simply a byproduct

of using PRT. Observers will often say things such as, "He used to be so disruptive and was spiraling downward, but now he is such a sweet child. I wonder what happened." The answer is simple: motivation.

THE SCIENCE BEHIND
DEALING WITH DISRUPTIVE BEHAVIOR

To understand why PRT is naturally suited for treating disruptive behavior, let's consider the case of a child who is being disruptive to avoid a difficult task. With PRT, the treatment for this behavior is to *motivate* the child to like the task so much that he or she does not want to avoid it. Think back to the discussion in Chapter 2 on the treatment of communication, when we conducted a study using PRT (called the Natural Language Paradigm in those early days) to teach first words to nonverbal children (R.L. Koegel et al., 1992). We compared two conditions. In one condition we incorporated the motivational procedures of PRT, and in the other condition we used a discrete trial format without the motivational

> ### *Common Functions of Disruptive Behavior*
> • Used to avoid a task
> • Used to escape a task
> • Used to gain attention
> • Used to obtain a desired item

principles. Do you remember what happened? The results showed unambiguously that when the motivational procedures were used, disruptive behavior either went away completely or was greatly reduced. We weren't even targeting disruptive behavior directly. This "side effect" makes a big difference, because with the disruptive behavior gone, the intervention providers can focus their efforts on teaching, rather than on constantly having to deal with the disruptive behavior (saying things such as "Put your hands down" or

"Stop screaming"). Think of the benefits in a school setting. How many times have you seen children with autism removed from the classroom or placed in "time-out" because they were disruptive? This "solution" often simply rewards the children's disruptive behaviors—especially if the function of the disruptive behavior was to escape or avoid a task.

Likewise, in another study we focused on teaching speech sounds to children who had such poor articulation that they were unintelligible (R.L. Koegel, Camarata, Koegel, Ben-Tall, & Smith, 1998). During the sessions, we unexpectedly found similar results with regard to the disruptive behavior. Prior to starting the study we had to get a human subject's approval. This means that we had to get special approval to

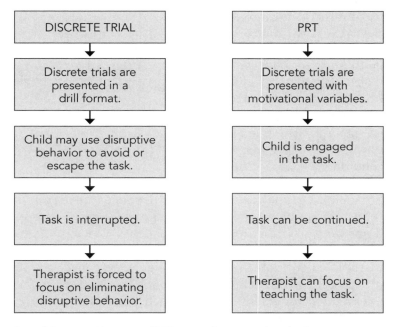

Pivotal Response Treatment (PRT) versus discrete trial methods.

conduct an experiment that involved people; this requirement is there because of past abuses, which you've probably heard of, when unethical procedures (often medical) were performed without the consent of the participant. Anyway, for this study, in the request for the human subject's approval we wrote that because we were doing different types of intervention, we would terminate the sessions if the children became disruptive as a result of the teaching. When we were conducting the sessions, we found that in the regular discrete trial approach (without motivational variables incorporated), the children frequently engaged in disruptive behavior, and many of the sessions had to be terminated. In the PRT condition, the children almost never engaged in such disruptive behaviors. They enjoyed the tasks so much that they were actually motivated to engage in the teaching protocol—the last thing they wanted was to terminate one of the sessions. In fact, some parents told us that their children were really upset on holidays when they were told that the autism center was closed!

Ask Yourself

PARENTS

1. In what settings is my child exhibiting disruptive behavior, and are motivational components incorporated into those settings?
2. Is my child getting what he or she wants through exhibiting disruptive behavior?

TEACHERS

1. Is my curriculum motivating for my students so that the likelihood of disruptive behavior is low?

2. How could I change my teaching so that motivational components could be included into each and every activity so that my students are unlikely to engage in disruptive behaviors?

4

How to Teach the Pivotal Area of Self-Initiation

Other than requesting items from his teacher or parent, Russell rarely socializes on his own. He just seems totally uninterested in others, and it takes quite a bit of prompting to get him to interact with other children. He has a pretty good vocabulary, can respond with simple sentences, and understands quite a bit. Do you have any suggestions for helping him make friends?

In previous chapters, we discussed how to get expressive communication started using motivational procedures, and we talked about finding those special things that a child likes, creating opportunities for teaching, and providing natural reinforcers. In our experience, as many as 95% of children who are nonverbal prior to the start of intervention, but have these motivational components included in their intervention, become verbal if intervention begins before the age of 3. If intervention begins between the ages of 3 and 5, approximately 85%–90% of the children will become verbal. The statistics are lower (about 20% likelihood of becoming verbal) if the children are nonverbal and begin intervention after the age of 5. But that doesn't mean that it's hopeless if your child is 5 and still nonverbal. About 20% still respond well, and the rest can usually learn to communicate with a good augmentative program that incorporates motivational strategies.

Now, if a child with autism is well on his way to using verbal communication regularly, it's probably true that, like most children with autism, he is using communication on a limited basis. Most of his communication use is probably for requests, which makes sense because that's what he's been taught. He now knows that every time he wants something, he has to use those good words or has to at least make a genuine word attempt. Other times children with autism will use communication for protests. They may say "No" if they don't want to engage in a task or "Bye-bye" if they've just had enough of social interaction. But that's about it. Most of the time when the children communicate, it's either a request or a protest. Engaging in communication just for the social pleasure of it isn't always something they pick up by themselves. Here's where teaching initiations comes in.

Before we start with the nuts and bolts of how to teach initiations, let's talk in general about initiations. Typically developing kids begin using initiations at a young age—very young. Even prelinguistic children will initiate interactions with their parents by pointing, looking at items, then looking back to their parents, and so forth—interactions we rarely see in children with autism.

Sometime around the first birthday, or shortly thereafter, typically developing language learners start pointing to things and saying "Dat?" The expression "Dat?" usually appears within a child's very first group of words. They may pick it up because adults have regularly shown them items and said "What's that?" to them, encouraging them to start labeling these items. Because they haven't learned how to combine words yet, the utterance is greatly simplified and comes out as a single word. However, the effect is the same. When a little child says "Dat?" to an adult, while pointing or looking at an item, the adult will label the item for him or her. In turn, the little child begins to develop a huge vocabulary. The interesting thing is that this happens without any specific training or teaching, with almost every typi-cally developing language learner. These basic questions, which start very early on, are social, and they are child initi-ated. In fact, some children do so many of these initiations that they develop absolutely huge vocabularies, and if their parents are responsive and label the item, and then add a little more information, they will begin learning language (how to combine words), too. For example, let's take little Brittany, a typically developing child who has been pointing for many months but who now points to an unusual item on the table and says, "Dat?" Mom or dad labels the item for her, saying, "Candle." Little Brittany responds with an approximation for the word, such as "cadow." Mom or dad may then say, "Yes, honey, it's a tall candle; it's a big, tall candle," thereby not only providing her with the label of the item but also helping to expand her language development. And so it goes in the world of typically developing language learners.

But there's a problem for children with autism spec-trum disorders. Surprisingly, most don't develop these initiations. This may be because we haven't taught them to use communication in this way. Remember, we started out teaching them to request highly desired items. But an-other reason may be that this type of initiation is very social, which makes the interaction a challenge to children with autism. In contrast, many typically developing children will repeatedly ask "Dat?" even if they already know the label of items, just for the social interaction. Thus, children who have a social communication disability—who find it diffi-cult to learn words and even more difficult to engage in so-cial interactions—may not be inclined to start a social and verbal interaction just for the fun of it. Whatever the reason, these children either aren't using these verbal initiations at all or not using them enough to sound like good conversa-tionalists. To make matters worse, they aren't learning the

Description of initiations

Initiation	Goal	Procedure	Example
What's that?	Increase lexicon and expressive vocabulary	Place a variety of desired objects in an opaque bag and prompt child to initiate "What's that?" Pull out an item and label it for the child. Gradually add in items the child can't label and fade out the bag.	The child likes dinosaurs, so put various dinosaurs inside a bag. Prompt the child to say "What's that?" Respond by saying "It's a T-rex!" while giving the child the toy. Later, place neutral items in the bag and fade out the bag.
Where is it?	Produce a generalized acquisition of prepositions	Hide a variety of desired items (e.g., in, under, inside, on, behind) and prompt child to initiate "Where is it?" Respond with the location so the child can obtain the desired object.	Have the child begin working on a puzzle of choice while you hide a few pieces around the room. Prompt the child to say "Where is it?" when looking for a piece. Reply with different prepositional phrases, such as "Under the table," so the child can find the desired piece.
Whose is it?	Develop the use of possessives, including yours and mine	Place desired items in front of the child and prompt the child to ask "Whose is it?" Respond with "It's yours." Then prompt the child to say "It's mine" and give the child the desired item.	Place the child's favorite candy on the table. Prompt the child to say "Whose is it?" and respond with "It's yours!" Prompt child to say "It's mine" and then give child the candy.

Initiation	Goal	Procedure	Example
What's happening?	Increase verb diversity and tense markers	Find pop-up books related to the child's interests and manipulate the tabs. Prompt the child to initiate the question in response to actions occurring ("What's happening?") or actions that have occurred ("What happened?").	The child likes trains, so build a train track and leave one piece broken. Prompt the child to say "What happened?" when the train gets to the broken track. Respond with "It broke!" and fix the track so that the child can continue.
Look!	Initiate attention-seeking phrases	Find toys or activities that the child enjoys and prompt her to say "Look!" to another person before giving her the toy or allowing her to engage in the activity.	The child enjoys shooting basketballs. Hold the ball and prompt child to say "Look!" to a peer. After the peer looks or says "Cool!" step aside so the child can throw the ball.
Help!	Initiate assistance-seeking phrases	Find toys or activities that the child will need help setting up. Prompt the child to say "Help!" and then help set up the toy or activity. Fade the prompt so that the child is saying "Help!" independently.	The child loves to draw, so put pens and paper on the table. Prompt the child to say "Help!" when he is trying to open a pen. Respond with "Sure, I'll help!" and open the pen. Give the pen to the child so he can draw.

many, all-important words and other linguistic pieces of information a child gains by asking questions.

Another problem is long-term outcomes. We did some research a while ago in which we looked back at preschool videotapes of young adults and adolescents with autism. We accidentally came upon this idea when we were in the midst of moving from one building to another. We had boxes upon boxes of old videotapes. The tapes were old and big—made long before cameras had shrunk to a size that could be easily thrown into a purse or bag. In fact, our tapes were so old that we didn't even have monitors on which we could watch them anymore. We were walking across campus one day when we started discussing what we should do with the tapes, and we got to chatting about the kids who were on them. Lynn's view was that we had history in those boxes and that the children on those tapes were now adults, so they were priceless. Bob started recalling old stories about the kids whose education had been a matter of blood, sweat, and tears, literally—the ones who had comprehensive programs around the clock with parent education, school coordination, and daily therapy at the university with the best-known, state-of-the-art intervention. They had all the indicators that made us optimistic about their futures. They were verbal and their IQs were above 50—two long agreed-upon indicators for a good prognosis. Some had excellent preacademic skills, and all had devoted and determined parents. Many of these children grew up to be adults with no symptoms of autism.

But what happened with Chance? And Sandy? And Larry? Something went terribly wrong. We didn't know why, but these children ended up in very restricted living conditions requiring constant supervision; they were aggressive, disruptive, or completely nonsocial and were not a part of inclusive community activities. How did Chance, who could read at age 3, end up lethargic and unable to succeed at a work skills program that taught menial jobs? How did Sandy, who could play the piano as well as any professional, come to be placed in a residential home that had constant supervision, and why had he become so aggressive that he couldn't leave the home? Why was Larry—highly verbal and fully included as a young child—now so disruptive that his parents couldn't take him out? We disagreed about what could have happened, but we did agree that their intervention programs had failed them. At the same time we discussed the children who—according to our memories— had exactly the same characteristics as preschoolers and the same intervention programs but had done so well. Jake gave the speech at his high school graduation, had a best friend, and loved team sports. Tyson was off to college after receiving excellent grades and being ranked as one of the top tennis players in California. And Lindsey was a popular kid all through high school, liked to babysit, posted movie reviews on the Internet, and scored the job she really wanted as a legal assistant. The question loomed before us: Why had these children had such vastly different outcomes when it seemed we did everything the same for all of them and when all of the children were, at least in our recollections, bright little preschoolers who were all progressing nicely in intervention and who should have all succeeded?

This is how our quest to find out what had happened to make these kids *so* different as adults began. For our review, we purposely picked children with wildly different long-term outcomes, either extremely positive or extremely poor. The kids who had the really positive outcomes were either working or going to college, had lots of friends, went to sleepovers and birthday parties, talked on the phone, and so forth. They basically had very few to no symptoms of autism. In contrast, the individuals who had the poor outcomes were living in segregated settings, had no unpaid companions or friends, were unemployed, did not go to college (most didn't even finish high school), and, for the most part, required constant supervision. Of course, there were varying degrees of outcomes in between these outliers; it's just that to answer our question, we were most interested in contrasting these groups on the far ends of the continuum to see what we could learn.

We had all the videos transferred to new tapes so that they could be watched and scored. Once that was accomplished, we began evaluating the tapes. Remember now, all the children were verbal before the age of 5, had IQs above 50, and were beginning to combine words to make short sentences. We looked at just about every variable you could imagine—play, self-stimulatory behavior, responsiveness, communication, and so forth. As the data began unfolding, we realized that although all of the children were bright and would answer if someone approached them, there was one clear and significant difference between the children with the poor outcomes and the children with the good outcomes. Specifically, the children with the more positive outcomes initiated more interactions with their parents. They brought their parents toys and other items from around the room as an invitation to play with them. They verbally initiated interactions with their parents or pointed to items to get their parents' attention. They were clearly different in their spontaneous self-initiations with their parents when they were in preschool. The poor-outcome group was deceptive, because they readily responded when someone initiated with them. However, when we looked closer, we saw that they just didn't initiate many—or any—interactions. And this seemed to make all the difference. It pointed to the fact that a child's intervention program may need to include active encouragement of initiations, especially if he or she isn't using any.

The next step was to test our theory. We decided to choose a group of children who had the same preinterven-

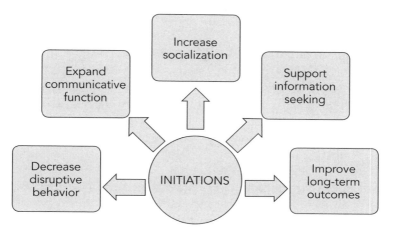

Collateral effects of initiations.

tion characteristics as the poor-outcome group—that is, verbal, IQ over 50, and beginning to combine words—then teach them an array of initiations, and see if they would also have positive long-term outcomes.

We brainstormed the intervention and decided to start with teaching the children to ask "What's that?" because it is such an early form in typically developing children and because it was clearly lacking in the children on our old tapes. We started out using storybooks, thinking it would be easy for parents to go through books and label pictures of items on the pages. But that was a total disaster. The children didn't ask the question, and they didn't even seem to be enjoying the activity at all. We tried this routine day after day for a week or two, but we never could get them to be enthusiastic about this activity. We started discussing the problem at home one night, and Bob suggested that we use something more motivational in the activity. So we went back to the drawing board. We thought and thought about how the activity could be more fun. Finally, we decided to try gathering up a whole bunch of a child's favorite toys and then placing them in an opaque bag. In this way, when we prompted the child to ask "What's that?" we could pull some highly desired item out of the bag. Thus, instead of the activity being totally social (and stressful) in nature, the child would get something she really liked from the bag, and perhaps she would think, "Hey, these initiations aren't so bad, after all!" Well, that worked, and the children began asking the question either during the first session or shortly thereafter. On occasion, it took longer, maybe 10 or 12 sessions, but most of the kids started asking the questions within the first few sessions. Interestingly, some of the children were so used to adults asking *them* the question "What's that?" that they kept trying to answer the question. They would say "bag" or "candy" or something they thought we had in the bag. But even the children who struggled in the beginning eventually began using the question. After they were consistently asking the question for about four sessions, we faded out our prompt and instead provided a short pause for the children to ask the question without a prompt.

Next, we started fading out the desired items and fading in neutral items that they didn't know how to label. After every third desired item, we added a neutral item. After a few sessions, we dropped this interval to every second item, then every other item, and then we started pulling out only items that they didn't know how to label. Finally, we faded out the bag so the children were asking "What's that?" about things in their natural environment that they couldn't label.

This worked. We collected data in the children's natural environments and discovered that they were using the newly learned question (which for many was the first question they had ever asked in their lives) in school and at home with their parents. In addition, we were overjoyed to find out that the questioning was leading to greatly improved

Here a child's initiation of the question "What's that?" can produce meaningful teaching interactions that can benefit the child.

vocabularies in all the children. We regularly assessed them to find words they didn't know and incorporated those vocabulary items into the intervention, interspersed with their favorite items. Any item that they couldn't label was used as a neutral (and targeted) vocabulary word during the intervention sessions. We were pleased that the children had added a new function to their language capabilities—beyond requests and protests—and were now using an information-seeking question. Their expanding vocabularies were a wonderful bonus.

Once the children were using "What's that?" on a regular basis, we moved on to a second question. (Unfortunately, they hadn't spontaneously begun using any of the other question forms following the teaching of the first question.) We started teaching them how to ask "Where is it?" which developmentally comes in shortly after "What's that?" in typically developing language learners. To do this, we again gathered the child's favorite items and hid them in strategic locations that corresponded to prepositions that the child didn't have in his or her repertoire. For example, one child craved Gummi Bear candies, so we bought the teeny, tiny Gummi Bears and hid them in various locations, such as *under* the cup, *behind* the toy car, *inside* the purse, or on *top* of the dollhouse. We then prompted the child to ask "Where is it?" and once he did, we told him the location and let him go find the treat in the specified location. The children acquired the second question even faster than the first, and most were asking it within the first session.

The third question we taught was "Whose is it?" We did this by putting together a group of the child's favorite things—little toys, candies, or anything else she liked. When she asked "Whose is it?" we responded with "Yours!" But she couldn't have the desired item we were holding up unless she reversed the pronoun and replied with "Mine!" Pronoun reversal is a huge problem for children with autism, so this is a perfect way to add another question, while having the child practice learning how to reverse pronouns. Once the children were asking "Whose" questions at a high frequency (remember, they were getting their favorite items when they did), we began interspersing more neutral items, such as a purse, pen, paper, or something they didn't particularly want for themselves, and replying with "Mine!" when they asked. To get back to the desired items, they had to respond with "Yours!" and the item immediately got placed aside in a pile of the communicative partner's items. This same procedure also works with the possessive "s" ending, such as Mommy's or Daddy's or Lynn's. We intersperse items associated with particular members of the family, friends, or the therapist with their desired things. Then, when we go through the items, they're learning the possessive endings.

Child initiations also work with verbs. We noticed that a lot of children with autism don't use many verbs, and even if they do, they sometimes don't use the *-ing* endings or past tense. Their language samples suggest that they can manage during simple conversation by using just a few verbs, but they usually don't have a large enough repertoire of verbs to sound natural during conversation. We started looking for "pop-up" books related to the children's interests—trucks, trains, bugs, animals—whatever they really liked. Then, depending on their target behavior, we manipulated the tabs of the pop-up book and taught them to ask "What's happening?" (while we continuously manipulated the tab) or "What happened?" (after we stopped manipulating the tab). We provided them with the verb and the appropriate verb ending. If they wanted, we let them play with the tab of the book after they repeated the verb. The children were learning these important questions, which are great for conversation, and at the same time their repertoire of verbs was expanding and their grammatical structures were improving.

Last, we taught the children to initiate "Look!" and "Help!" These expressions provide the child with a way to get attention and a way to get assistance. "Help!" in particular is an important, if not critical, function to learn. Kids get frustrated, they find things challenging, and they need assistance with many things. Just spend one lunch period on the playground and try opening those spill-proof containers, and you'll get a feel for their daily frustrations. To deal with frustrations and difficult situations, many children with autism become disruptive. We've seen it in many, many classrooms: A child becomes disruptive because an assignment is difficult or an activity is challenging; the teacher comes over, prompts the child to say "Help me!" and then helps the child with whatever problem is at hand; and the child eventually calms down. What's really happening in this scenario? The child has *learned* a clear chain of behaviors: First,

I whine, cry, or do something disruptive to get the teacher's attention when there's a problem. Second, the teacher will come over. Third, the teacher will prompt me to say "Help!" And fourth, voila! I've gotten the help I wanted. This is not the correct chain. The goal is for the children to initiate the appropriate verbal request "Help!" when they need it, not when they are prompted.

Now, let's talk about the collateral behaviors that happen when we teach initiations. First, disruptive behaviors decrease—that's nice because you don't even have to target them directly. Second, the initiations provide another communicative function for the child. That is, beyond requesting items and activities and protesting, the child now has information-seeking strategies in his repertoire. Children learn important information from these initiations. Next, an initiation is social, so this step has the effect of making the child more social. Think about it—an asocial child isn't going to want to start a social-verbal interaction. And finally, the long-term outcomes are far better when the child regularly initiates interaction. Thus, initiations are a pivotal area.

EMPIRICAL EVIDENCE FOR THE IMPORTANCE OF INITIATIONS

What really matters in successful treatment is the long run, and studies show that initiations may be critical to very positive, long-term outcomes. This is why lots of researchers have focused on the pivotal area of social initiations. If you take a look at typically developing children, you can get an idea of how many different initiations there are and how often they use them. In fact, typically developing children begin to initiate interactions very early in life. Before they are even 1 year old, they will look at an item that interests them, then at another person, then back at the item. This is called joint attention. Children both initiate and respond to these types of interactions: If you point out something to them, they'll usually respond by looking back and forth between the interesting item and you. Unfortunately, children with autism spectrum disorders don't do this or rarely do it (e.g., Mundy & Newell, 2007; Mundy & Sigman, 2006; Sheinkopf, Mundy, Claussen, & Willoughby, 2004; Travis, Sigman, & Ruskin, 2001; Vaughan Van Hecke et al., 2007). Joint attention is very important, even pivotal, in many ways. First, it is social. It is how children interact before they have words.

Joint Attention

Sharing interest in an event or object by pointing or gazing back and forth between the item and another individual

And joint attention is a precursor to first words. Joint attention involves making eye contact, sharing pleasure, communicating, and socializing. All these areas are more difficult for children with autism spectrum disorders.

Not only do children with autism lack the ability to engage in joint attention, but they also seem to develop very limited ways of using language. That is, they almost never use language that initiates social interaction. As a whole, the bodies of research discussed in this section suggest that the lack of initiations may be a pivotal problem that results in seriously atypical development. For example, Wetherby and Prutting (1984) showed that children with autism use communication almost exclusively for either protests (such as saying "No," "Go away," or "Bye-bye"), which are incredibly effective ways of limiting or terminating social interactions (Lynn even worked with one child who routinely "fired" people!) or requests for reinforcers (such as items or actions), which can become fairly sophisticated (such as "I want cookie, please"). However, these types of language interactions provide minimal, if any, opportunity for *social* learning. For the most part, in a teaching interaction, a child with autism is responding to an initiation from an adult.

The spontaneous language of children with autism contains very few, if any, social initiations by the children themselves and almost no questions asked for the purpose of social curiosity or seeking information from others.

Because children with autism don't generally use social initiations, we are led to some other important concepts, such as the idea of curiosity. In one important study, O'Neill (1987) placed many boxes full of interesting things around a living room. When typically developing children were brought into the room, they followed social norms and didn't open any of the boxes, reporting that they thought they were gifts and that they shouldn't be opened. However, they did play with and explore every other item in the room and explored every area of the room. In contrast, when children with autism were taken into the room, they opened one or a few of the boxes and played exclusively with those few items. They did not explore the rest of the room, nor did they play with or explore any other items in the room. This study showed that children with autism, compared to their typically developing peers, engaged in few social norms, tended to interact with fewer items, and shifted less often among items than did typically developing children. These wildly different results suggested that children with autism exhibit a deficit in curiosity and that they might benefit greatly from interventions that could teach or motivate curiosity and inquisitiveness.

Theories about the importance of getting the children to initiate were addressed to some extent in early studies. For example, many researchers explored the idea of teaching question asking as an attempt to teach generalized imitation with various populations of individuals with disabilities (e.g., Guess, Sailor, & Baer, 1978; Guess, Sailor, Rutherford, & Baer, 1968; Twardosz & Baer, 1973). These researchers hoped that imitation might be a launch pad for development. Although this early work had huge implications from a theoretical point of view, the generalized use of question asking was more elusive in children with autism. That is, although the children were able to learn many new behaviors through generalized imitation and question asking, they did not appear to be motivated to ask questions in their natural environments. Possibly because of this limitation, very little research was done on question asking for children with autism over the next several decades.

There were, however, a few studies that showed very promising results with individuals with autism (e.g., Hung, 1977; Taylor & Harris, 1995). Once again, the results suggested that the children could learn to ask questions and, under some conditions, could be prompted to generalize their question asking; however, there was no indication that the children were motivated to ask questions or to seek information without specific prompting. But this line of research was very important. It provided a foundation for future studies that would focus on the generalized use of question asking. The motivational components of PRT proved to be a way to accomplish this task. That is, when motivational components were used within the intervention, the children began asking questions for information-seeking purposes alone—an important developmental milestone. The results also suggested the importance of motivating the children to initiate social interactions that might improve their social development.

In an early study incorporating the all-important motivational components, we taught children with autism to ask "What's that?" (L.K. Koegel et al., 1998). We chose this question because most typically developing children begin using this question ("Dat?") in their first year of life—often within their first group of words. When a parent or care provider labels the indicated item, they begin to accumulate vocabulary words. Thus, we asked two questions: Can children with autism learn to initiate toward others by asking information-seeking questions, and does asking such questions lead to their acquisition of new knowledge? The children in this first study were specifically chosen because they rarely or never used any questions. However, by incorporating the motivational components, this research showed that the children could indeed learn to ask "What is it?" and when they did so, their vocabularies increased as adults answered the questions by labeling the objects in question. However, most important, the study showed not only that the children learned to ask questions but also that they were motivated to ask questions in other community environments. For example, the children began asking "What's that?" about items they didn't know how to label at school and at home, thus providing learning opportunities beyond their direct therapy interactions. This was the hoped-for result, and it appeared as though incorporating the motivational components was the key to creating a "love of learning" or a positive association with the question so that it would become a frequent and natural part of their interactions. The research showed that the children could become motivated to ask questions for the purpose of seeking information and that this question asking might result in therapeutic gains throughout the day, even outside of the therapy sessions.

Anecdotally, the questions also appeared to be important for more than gaining new vocabulary words; the new skill also helped to reduce disruptive behaviors. For example, one child wanted a granola bar that was stored on a high shelf far out of his reach. Unfortunately, he did not know the term "granola bar." He initially began to have a tantrum and cry, and his mother had no idea why he was becoming so upset. Then he stopped, pointed up to the box, and asked "What is it?" His mother then replied, "It's a granola bar." He proceeded to say, "I want granola bar." Prior to being taught the "What is it?" question at 3½ years old, he had never asked a question in his life. Thus, not only did his vocabulary increase, but through the use of questions, he also became less frustrated and therefore less disruptive. It appeared that question asking might have some very widespread impacts for increased learning opportunities in the children's natural, everyday settings, as well as implications for broader impacts on the children's behavior as a whole. Thus, we began further work to see whether different types of social initiations, and especially question asking, might be an important new pivotal area.

In a second study, we tried using the motivational procedures that worked so well with teaching "What's that?" with another question (L.K. Koegel et al., 2010). Before the intervention, the children never asked "where" questions, even though they all had large vocabularies and could combine words into little sentences. The data showed that, similar to the first study, the children could easily and rapidly learn to ask "Where is it?" and when they did so, their acquisition of prepositions increased without the need for any additional training specifically focused on prepositions. They also had fun during the intervention, because it included motivational components. When they asked "Where is it?" to find out the location of, for example, a Gummi Bear, the parent might answer, "It is *in* the lunch box," and they got to find and eat the treat. Under those conditions, the children learned the prepositions (e.g., *in*). Again, many became less disruptive when they could independently initiate questions in situations that would previously have caused them frustration.

In a third group of studies on question asking, L.K. Koegel, Carter, et al. (2003) studied the questions "What's happening?" and "What happened?" Again, the data showed that children with autism rarely asked such questions and used a very, very small number of verbs. As with the other questions, the data showed that the children could easily learn to ask these additional questions and, when they did, their acquisition of verbs increased, as did their use of the correct verb ending (e.g., -*ing* or past tense). That is, when they asked "What's happening?" parents and others usually answered by using a verb, and the children with autism acquired these verb meanings without the need for additional teaching. That really saved a lot of time.

As the studies began to accumulate, we once again began to wonder whether the procedures could somehow be combined. As we had during the original research in the area of motivation, we wondered whether this new method could be integrated into an intervention package that taught many different types of initiations. We hypothesized that such a package might have a particularly powerful effect on learning and development and could become pivotal with respect to intervention. To test this hypothesis, we did a two-part study (L.K. Koegel et al., 1999).

In the first part, we looked at children who had very different outcomes after receiving very similar interventions for many years. Videotapes of two groups of preschool children were analyzed for differences in their pretreatment characteristics. One group of children eventually had extremely good long-term outcomes, and the other group had extremely poor long-term outcomes. When we examined the children who had poor outcomes, we found that at pretreatment those children exhibited only a few (or even no) social initiations. It is important to note that these low-initiating children had similar language ages and language test scores to the good-outcome children, and they had very intensive comprehensive interventions in their homes, clinics, and schools. The children in the positive-outcome group were different from the other group in only one major characteristic: They had exhibited many social initiations—one child made more than three initiations a minute—while playing with toys and interacting with their parents.

The above results, showing such dramatic differences between the groups, were particularly surprising because the children in the poor-outcome group did not look particularly different from the other group at intake. Overall, to the uninformed eye, the two groups appeared almost identical. For example, at pretreatment the children in both groups would answer questions appropriately, giving the impression that they were quite high functioning and should do pretty well with intervention. The difference at intake was that the children in the poor-outcome group were content playing or being alone unless someone initiated an interaction with them. They weren't the least bit social and were dependent upon others to learn anything. Although they did learn when others taught them, they did not learn anything outside of those specific treatment sessions. In contrast, the children who initiated interactions were setting up continual learning opportunities—by themselves—all day long. This behavior difference appeared to have a very great impact on overall success in the long term.

The differences between the two groups were extremely dramatic, suggesting that social initiations might be a particularly important pivotal area for intervention. Thus, we conducted a second phase to that study. This time we assessed the feasibility of teaching a variety of differ-

Here initiations between children can produce many positive academic and social learning opportunities.

ent social initiations to children who exhibited very few or no initiations. To replicate the first study, we identified a group of children with similar language ages and behaviors to the poor-outcome group of children in the first (descriptive) phase of the study. In this second phase of the study, we experimentally manipulated initiations by teaching the children how to engage in a wide variety of initiations. For example, we taught the children how to initiate different types of interactions, such as saying "Look!" to draw others' attention to things the children were doing and saying "Help!" when they were having difficulty with a task. We collected data over a period of many years and were pleased that at follow-up when the children were adolescents, their outcomes were similar to the high-initiating group in the descriptive first phase of the study. That is, these children, like those in the earlier study, developed friendships (and even had best friends), were invited to parties, went to sleepovers, made and received phone calls, were earning high grades in general education classrooms, and so forth. Exactly what we had hoped for.

Such results suggested that motivation is a critically important pivotal area for developing initiations. That is, all of the early work showed that the children were capable of developing initiations but that they were not motivated to initiate socially. The study by L.K. Koegel et al. (1999) suggested that the children could be motivated to initiate. If true, it meant that the children might begin showing initiated joint attention (looking back and forth between the communication partner and some indicated object) without any direct treatment. Bruinsma (2004) and Vismara and Lyons (2007) tested this idea. Both studies used PRT to establish motivation and then assessed whether joint attention would occur without any direct treatment. In both studies, joint attention did emerge spontaneously in approximately two months after motivation was established through PRT.

Further, in the Vismara and Lyons (2007) study, the children immediately showed joint attention with respect to favorite objects that they were motivated to play with from the beginning, another indication that motivation is a pivotal area for development.

In another study, we tested this motivational issue in a different way (R.L. Koegel et al., 2009). We embedded social components into rewards that were given to the children (e.g., if the child liked to bounce on a trampoline for a reward, then another person would bounce on the trampoline with the child to make the activity social). By embedding the social component into the rewarding aspects of the activities, the children became highly motivated to initiate further social interactions. Thus, they learned the target behaviors being taught to them, and they also became motivated to initiate social interactions.

Taken together, the above research suggests that motivation is pivotal in establishing social initiations. Once motivation is an integral part of the teaching, social initiations of many different types can be taught, with the desired collateral effect of long-term positive outcomes on development. This time motivation was an underlying and critical component to the performance of a second pivotal behavior, initiations. And initiations seemed to be extremely important for acquisition of a variety of types of new knowledge as well as for the development of linguistic and social competence.

*M*yth: Children with autism will pick up a variety of communicative functions as they get older without direct intervention.

*R*eality: Without intervention, children with autism spectrum disorders tend to use communication solely for requests and protests.

*M*yth: Individuals on the spectrum prefer to be alone.

*R*eality: Most individuals on the spectrum report that they desire friendships and intimate relationships, yet they do not initiate social interactions without intervention.

*R*eality: Individuals with autism can be motivated to want to initiate social interactions.

*R*eality: With motivational intervention, children with autism initiate many types of interactions, with many types of broad collateral gains, without the necessity of the presence of a treatment provider in every setting.

MAKING IT WORK IN EVERYDAY SETTINGS

Now that you understand the importance of initiations, let's talk about how to get them started in everyday settings—at home, at school, and in the community.

Prompting Questions in Children

If you aren't hearing your student or child using questions very often—or at all—start taking time every day to work on this. Throw something interesting in your purse or glove compartment every day and prompt the child to ask "What's in there?" or "What's that?" on the way home from school. Get a brown bag out of the cupboard and fill it with fun things and prompt him to ask "What's that?" In an inclusive classroom setting with typically developing children, make a bag full of things for the class or for each student to ask about during circle time. Then gradually fade the desired items as the child begins enjoying asking the questions. Hide favorite items so that the child has to ask "Where is it?" or play a game with special items or treats hidden around the house or classroom. Make sure that at any given time, whether at school or at home, you are working on at least one initiation.

The important attention-getting initiations "Look!" and "Help!" can make a big difference in a child's life. You might be thinking to yourself "Why would a child with autism want to get attention? They usually want to get *rid* of people!" Well, that is sometimes true, but remember that everything you have been doing has focused on motivation, so now the child should be realizing that even though this "talking thing" is difficult, it leads to desired outcomes. Nearly every time. This changes everything. It isn't pointless hard work or drill practice; this is not so bad (even if it is difficult) if something good comes out of it! Even when you've worked on something that is social—like question asking—you have taught it in such a way that it's rewarding. And that's exactly the way you can teach the child to use "Look!" The easiest way to teach "Look!" is to find activities or items the child really enjoys. This can be sliding down the slide, letting a toy car go down a ramp, or getting a favorite treat. Again, anything the child enjoys. But this time, before giving a desired item to the child or letting her engage in her favorite activity, you're going to prompt her to say "Look, Mommy!" "Look, Daddy!" or "Look, Susie!" Then, quickly give her the item or let her do the activity after she calls attention to it. Remember, if you are prompting this, *don't— please don't*—turn it into a task. If after she says "Look!" you start turning it into a test by saying "What color is it?" or "How do you spell *car*?" then she probably won't draw your attention to the item in the future. Simply say "Wow! A treat!" or "Cool, a car!" then let her have it. In fact, this is the case with all of the questions. If the child asks you "What is it?" just answer. Don't respond with "What do you think it is?" Likewise, if you label the item after he says "What's that?" and then begin a line of questioning, such as "What are you going to do with the hammer?" you may totally lose him. Make it easy, make it simple, and don't turn it into a demanding situation. When children begin initiating interactions, everything is fragile. To keep their motivation high, the whole social communicative interaction needs to be pleasant.

In teaching "Help!" the idea is to set up situations that are a teeny bit frustrating—but not to the point of triggering disruptiveness—and then prompt the child to request "Help!" Once the child is responding to your prompt, you begin fading that prompt by either saying part of the word "He...," or providing a pause, or looking expectantly so that the child uses "Help!" on her own. If you practice this word frequently, then eventually it will become "automatic" and will be used readily when an activity is frustrating or challenging. You may still need to ignore the disruptive behavior if it occurs on occasion, but the child will have a nice, appropriate behavior to use in these situations.

Improving Conversation in Children, Adolescents, and Adults

For older children, adolescents, and adults, question asking is the key to improving social conversation. Many adolescents and adults with autism or Asperger syndrome have difficulty engaging in social conversation—either getting it started or keeping it going. Almost all of them have difficulty with question asking, and that's why there are long, awkward pauses and one-sided conversations. We've been working with adolescents and adults on conversation, using either self-management or video self-modeling. Teaching question asking has been very helpful for improving social conversation. In practice sessions, we provide very specific statements that invite a question. We call these "leading statements." For example, we might say "I had a great lunch today!" and then pause. Prior to intervention, the pause usually continues for a long time. For intervention, we either stop the conversation at an appropriate time (e.g., when there is a long pause) or, when viewing tapes after a session, we pause the tape. We then ask the student, "Do you think there is a question you could have asked here?" If needed, we provide suggestions. For example, with the "lunch" leading statement, we might say, "In that situation you may want to ask 'What did you have?' or 'Where did you go?' which will keep the conversation going." Lots of common leading statements can be practiced, such as "I had a great weekend," "I went on a great vacation last summer," "I'm doing something interesting this weekend," "I'll be out of town next week," and so forth. These leading statements easily lend themselves to a variety of questions that might be asked. We usually begin by giving a variety of suggestions about possible questions, and then we fade our prompting by asking the individual if she can come up with questions that might be good to ask that relate to the conversational partner's statements. Often we need to give feedback on the appropriateness of the questions, and sometimes the questions don't seem to be at all related to the previous topic of conversation. This feedback is important because to be a good conversational partner, the person with autism or Asperger syndrome must learn to be a good listener and must be able to respond in such a way that the partner knows the person is listening, interested, and empathetic to the conversational partner's topics.

Of course, the flip side of conversational responses is conversational initiations, and a question is a great way to start a conversation. Any number of common topics will work, such as asking about hobbies, local events, news events, books read, a job, and so forth. Also, some contexts lend themselves to related questions, such as going to a bookstore, museum, or sporting event. Individuals on the spectrum need to be able to begin a conversation by initiating a question or making a relevant comment. And, as always, it is important to practice these questions in natural settings. When working with adults, we take them to local events, restaurants, bars, coffee shops, or wherever they might enjoy going. For high schoolers, we have student volunteers come from other local schools to practice social conversation, attend school events (e.g., sports games, dances), and go on community outings with them. The involvement of new people is critical, because the newly learned conversational skills don't always generalize from one person to others. But with time and practice, most students become significantly better conversationalists, which helps make dating and hanging out with friends a reality, not just a dream.

Meli was a darling 4-year-old girl who had never asked a question, despite the fact that she had a fairly large vocabulary, could make short little sentences like "I want a cookie, please," knew all her letters, and could count to 100. We decided that questions would greatly improve her communication, so we set forth toward that goal. But in Meli's case, we ran into an unusual problem when we tried to teach her to ask questions. We began by gathering her favorite items, which included a variety of squishy toys, red Gummi Bears (she wasn't interested in any other colors), LEGOs to build with, and small stuffed animals or figures of dogs. We placed them inside an opaque bag and began to teach her to ask questions about the bag, as we had done with countless other children. We first started prompting her to ask us "What's that?" as we reached in the bag, but she was so used to adults asking her to respond to that question that she said, "Bag!" then "Candy!" then "Dog!" After several unsuccessful attempts to name the items, we again tried to prompt her, "Meli, can you say 'What's that?'" She didn't respond at all. We tried again, but again she didn't respond. We then prompted her to say "Gummi Bear" and she immediately responded with "Gummi Bear." Hmmmmm. Now she was confusing us. So we tried again. Can you say "chair"? She responded with "chair." Can you say "desk"? She responded with "desk." Then we asked if she could say "sky." No response. And it went on like that.

It turned out that she would repeat anything that she could see but would not repeat anything that she couldn't see. Once we had that figured out, we began pointing to the bag and saying "That!" She did repeat "That!" so we pulled out one of her favorite items. We continued with "That!" until she readily said it and immediately got the desired items. Eventually, we added "What's" to the "That!" and she began repeating "What's that?" Her case was tricky, because it took longer than average to figure out what was going on and then to teach her the first question, but eventually she got it and almost immediately began using the question in all kinds of different places—school, the grocery store, at the baby sitter's house, and so forth. From then on, she progressed like the other children. But Meli illustrated an important point: One size does not fit all. People are all different, and the intervention needs to be tailored to the child.

Ask Yourself

PARENTS

1. Is my child using questions?
2. Is my child using enough questions that learning is occurring in everyday settings?

3. Is my child using a variety of questions?

4. Is my child initiating a variety of social interactions, such as asking me to look at things he or she has done?

TEACHERS

1. As a teacher, am I creating an environment in which questions are used frequently?

2. Am I responding to all of the questions my student asks?

3. Is my student using questions with peers?

4. Am I encouraging curiosity?

5. Am I encouraging interactions that are not demanding, so my student will want to initiate more interactions rather than avoiding them in the future?

II

How and When to Implement Treatment

5

Maximizing
Family Involvement

Benny turned 3 years old last month. He was diagnosed with autism when he was 2½; he said only a handful of words at that point, and he cried like crazy and threw some pretty wild tantrums—ending up face down on the ground and stiff as a board—when he was told "no," during transitions away from a desired activity, or at just about any other time when things didn't go his way. Although the insurance company paid for some of his ABA intervention sessions, his parents invested a fair amount of their savings in his treatment. First, they cleared out their basement for his sessions, painted the walls, and purchased new carpeting and furniture. They initially sat in on most of his sessions, but because he was so disruptive when they were there, his therapists asked them not to attend. His parents wanted to be with him so badly that they compromised and set up a video-recording system in their basement so they could watch the treatment at any time. Since his diagnosis, he has progressed steadily: He doesn't have tantrums as often, and he's learned additional words. His parents adore his therapists, but whenever the therapists leave, he reverts back to his old patterns of crying and tantrums. The parents feel they are fortunate to have therapists who provide intervention for Benny 40 hours a week, but he's still almost impossible the rest of the time. When they called us to consult, can you guess what our concern was?

We hope the answer was easy to figure out. The fact that Benny's parents were not a part of the intervention was wrong. *So* wrong. For so many reasons. For a child with autism to thrive, the parents need to learn a whole new set of parenting rules. Parenting techniques that work so well for typically developing children just *don't* work (usually) for children with autism. That's why it is critical that parents be part of the intervention process. Parents need to learn the strategies to help their child learn to communicate, become social, and play with other children. They need to learn how to implement these strategies throughout their child's waking hours and how to prompt many, many appropriate behaviors in natural settings.

Let's take Benny's example. Because all of the intervention was being implemented by therapists, Benny's parents were not learning any strategies to prompt important communicative and social behaviors. To make matters worse, Benny's intervention was being implemented solely at a small table in the basement. He wasn't learning to use his newly acquired behaviors in everyday, natural settings.

Teaching parents specialized procedures is especially important, because natural parenting procedures often don't

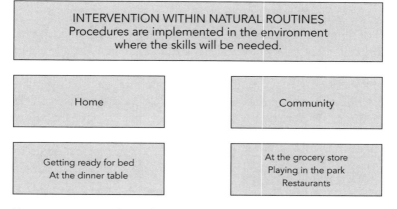

How intervention can be implemented within natural routines.

work with kids on the spectrum. Typically developing kids generally respond well to threats, the "countdown" ("I'm going to count to three, and you'd better have those toys picked up" or "I'm leaving, you'd better come now"), or time-out ("If you don't stop crying you're going to your room"). Once when we took our kids to the zoo, we heard a parent say, "If you don't stand in line properly, then that policeman over there is going to come over and get mad at you." Although this isn't a parent–child interaction we would recommend, it did work; the kid shaped up. However wrong that tactic was—not only because the parent couldn't follow through on the threat but also because kids need to learn that when parents say something they *mean it* (not that someone else will apply the consequence)—the truth is that typically developing children will often shape up when parents threaten them. Not so with children on the spectrum. Children with autism have difficulty with socialization, and children that aren't as social don't really care about what people think. So threatening a child with "People are looking at you making a scene" probably won't make the child shape up. So it is not just important, but critical, that parents learn the strategies that will help their child. In fact, anyone who spends any significant amount of time with a child with autism should also learn to use the procedures. That means auntie, uncle, grammie, granddad, the nanny, the baby sitter, the school aide, the school staff, and so forth. This broader approach means the child will have a more consistent and constant therapeutic environment across all of his waking hours. It also means that life as the parents knew it before they had a child with autism has completely changed. They need to create opportunities for learning on a continuous and ongoing basis—the child with autism usually won't approach them and ask them to teach him something. This means a complete lifestyle change—one that, as you will see throughout this book, can be a lot of fun for everyone.

If you are a teacher or a therapist, it is critically important that you work with your student's family on a regular— very regular—basis. The best way to help your student's family is through "practice with feedback." This means that you will need to demonstrate the intervention procedures and then have the parents implement the procedures while you give them feedback. This may mean having them follow through once they give their child a command, or it may mean showing them how to provide learning opportunities and incorporate motivational procedures into these opportunities. To create a seamless, round-the-clock intervention, the parents of your student will need to know what your target behaviors are as well as specific—very specific—ways to work on these behaviors. If your student's parents are busy and unable to make it to practice sessions, make sure you arrange contact in a different way, whether through regular phone calls, videotapes, home visits, notes sent home, or e-mails. The bottom line is that your student will perform much better if you and the parents coordinate goals and have consistent procedures for teaching these goals. Remember, if the parents pick goals that are important to them, they will be more likely to work on them. Even if you wouldn't select a particular goal yourself, if the goal is important to the family's

Family Involvement

Target behaviors:

- Involve parents in developing the target behaviors.
- Keep parents up to date on target behaviors and specific procedures for each behavior.
- Focus on children's strengths.

Demonstrate intervention:

- Involve parents in designing procedures.
- Demonstrate intervention procedures while describing each component.

Give feedback:

- Develop feedback consistent with the family's values, routines, and needs.
- Give positive feedback as well as areas for improvement.

cultural or personal values, it is important for you to work on it with them. Dr. Lynn Kern Koegel once worked with a preschool child who couldn't say the "v" sound. He had a lot of behaviors that she thought were much more important than the "v" sound, but his parents emphasized this one. His name was "David," and when anyone asked him his name he tried to reply but was always frustrated when the listener echoed his name incorrectly. Having David learn to say his name correctly was the top priority for his parents. Once we taught him how to say his name, his parents were excited and happy to work on his other behavior problems. So although we wouldn't have picked "v" as a first target behavior, it was of utmost importance to his family.

If you're a parent, don't let what happened to Benny's parents happen to you. Insist on participating in the sessions, or find a new program if you are excluded. It takes a village, it takes a team, and it takes the village and the team using a coordinated and consistent approach to achieve the best child outcomes. It's all about speeding up the learning process, and there's no doubt that more opportunities, under different circumstances, in different situations, and with different people will be the most helpful for the child with autism. Furthermore, intervention needs to be implemented throughout all of the child's waking hours—and even during sleeping hours if the child has a sleep disorder! So get everyone—*everyone*—together and onboard, and start creating a continuous and ongoing therapeutic environment for your child.

THE RESEARCH TO BACK IT: PARENT EDUCATION

Scientific discoveries do not generally come about at lightning-bolt speed. They are the result of careful planning and empirically based discoveries built upon a sound scientific foundation. Developing these treatment packages takes time. Taking the time for a scientific foundation is not a luxury; it's a necessity. Serious problems can occur when intervention providers rely on non–evidence-based approaches or even a combination of some scientifically sound and some not so scientifically sound approaches. Using that kind of approach puts you on shaky ground. The last thing you want is to be sitting on a witness stand testifying about your intervention, only to come out looking totally incompetent under cross-examination. We've seen that happen more than once.

One of the earliest, and perhaps most infamous, approaches to the treatment of autism was based upon a theory that had no supporting data whatsoever. In 1943, Kanner published a paper describing autism and suggested that the cause might be the cold and uncaring personality characteristics of the parents. This idea was later discussed in detail by Bruno Bettelheim in *The Empty Fortress: Infantile Autism and the Birth of the Self* (1967). The approach relied on psychoanalytic theory and proposed that parents caused their children to develop autism during infancy by using parenting practices that were traumatic to the child.

Those who followed this approach, which was widely accepted for many decades, felt that the parents of children with autism had psychological problems themselves and that they either purposefully or accidentally traumatized (or even tortured) their children. This psychoanalytic theory, which was very broadly publicized and was for decades the primary approach to the treatment of autism, caused severe distress for parents, who were told, and often believed, that they must be terrible people to have caused this severe disability in their beloved child.

This belief was an especially tragic misunderstanding, as scientific evidence eventually disproved the theory, showing that parents of children with autism did not have any greater levels of psychological problems than did parents of typically developing children (R.L. Koegel, Schreibman, O'Neill, & Burke, 1983). In the early days of our research, up until the early 1980s, it was very common for parents to come into our offices profoundly stressed and depressed because they had been told that they were the cause of their child's autism. One mother reported that when she asked her doctor what she could do for her child, he responded by saying, "You've done enough already," and proceeded to recommend that she place him in a mental institution.

*M*yth: Parents cause their child to develop autism.

*R*eality: Parents are the solution to their child's development.

Again, our early research, and that of others, found that almost all of the parents were completely typical, without any psychological problems of any type at all! Interestingly, subsequent research showed that parents most definitely were *not* the cause of autism and, further, that their help in delivering treatment is essential in their child's recovery. Thus, parent involvement and coordinated assistance in treatment delivery is listed as one of the major critical components of PRT.

To be specific, evidence-based approaches rapidly found that parents could play a critical role in helping their children make large gains. In an early study, Lovaas et al. (1973) noticed an interesting pattern in their long-term, follow-up data. Children were classified into two groups: those who were treated with intensive intervention in a residential hospital program and those who were treated in an outpatient clinic, which was not as intensive but which involved the parents in the intervention sessions. Two extremely interesting results relevant to this discussion emerged from this research. At posttesting, both groups of children had made considerable gains, and those gains were approximately equal for the two groups. This result surprised us, because the outpatient group had far fewer hours of intervention from a well-trained and highly skilled clinician. However, even more interesting was that at follow-up, after the children had completed the formal treatment, extremely large differences began to emerge between the two groups. Believe it or not, the group that had received intensive treatment 24 hours a day, 7 days a week, had lost almost all of their gains during the follow-up period after being discharged from the residential setting. In contrast, the children who had received less intervention, but whose parents served as assistants during the sessions, did not lose their gains and actually continued to improve further!

This was such an important finding, because it showed that the parents could, and did, continue to provide the treatment in the home setting based on what they had learned by assisting in the clinic sessions. This study led to widespread interest in researching different types of intervention packages that included systematic parent education components. We even had a project funded by the National Institute of Mental Health, in which one group of children got a clinician-delivered intervention and the other group got the same intervention delivered by the children's parents with support from a clinician (R.L. Koegel, Schreibman, Britten, Burke, & O'Neill, 1982). You might have already guessed that the results were consistent with the families in the study by Lovaas et al. (1973). We showed that when only a clinician delivered the intervention, there was improvement, but the children rarely used their newly learned behaviors with other people and in new settings. In fact, there was very poor long-term maintenance of gains. However, when parents assisted with the intervention, the children exhibited their gains in virtually every setting and also showed continued improvements over time.

We aren't the only group that has noticed this pattern. Researchers in a variety of independent laboratories have found the same thing. For example, when parents are trained in the Natural Language Paradigm version of PRT, the children's language and play improves (Gillett & LeBlanc, 2007). Also, Baker-Ericzén et al. (2007) found great benefits when parents—and they worked with hundreds of parents—were taught to work with their children with autism in community settings, also suggesting that widespread implementation of PRT was practical and plausible in community settings outside formal university centers. In another large-scale study, PRT was effectively imple-

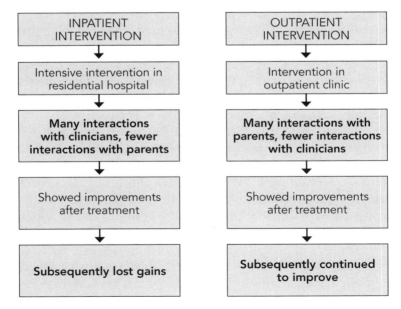

A comparison of inpatient and outpatient intervention programs.

mented in the context of a trainer-of-trainers model and on an extremely large scale (throughout the entire province of Nova Scotia in Canada) with both families and professionals working together (Bryson et al., 2007). Thus, PRT implemented in a coordinated team approach by parents and professionals is both effective and practical on a large scale.

There's more. In 1988, Laski, Charlop-Christy, and Schreibman published a study showing that parents could easily and rapidly learn PRT and could help their children make huge improvements. Perhaps even more interesting is that when parents were trained to deliver PRT, not only did their children show improvement, but there were also generalized improvements in the whole family's happiness and overall style of interactions (R.L. Koegel et al., 1996; Schreibman et al., 1991). That is, the parents have considerably higher affect—such as happiness and interest—when they use PRT compared to when they use a traditional, discrete trial approach using a drill-practice format. We also showed that the entire pattern of family interactions improves when parents use PRT. And this happens outside treatment times as well, such as at dinnertime. They interact with their children in more relaxed ways, showing an overall improvement in happiness for the entire family.

In an interesting extension of this line of research, we demonstrated that parents living in areas remote from a treatment center could be taught to use PRT during an intensive, week-long intervention program and that, consequently, their children showed behavioral gains as well as gains in happiness (R.L. Koegel, Symon, & Koegel, 2002). Further, the parents also improved in their overall levels of happiness. This result was even more impressive, because the gains were still apparent after the families returned to their home communities—often far, far away, where no treatment provider was available. Thus, this study showed at least two major benefits of family involvement: First, parents can successfully provide PRT intervention and produce behavioral improvements in their children even in communities far away from an intervention center. Second, after the families participated in the full-time, parent education program for a week, the overall levels of happiness of the children and their parents improved as well. An unexpected surprise was that the parents who were trained in PRT often trained other individuals (e.g., teachers) in their home communities, extending the benefits well beyond what they personally gained in that week (Symon, 2005).

These positive results show that, unequivocally, parents should be included as a formal part of treatment teams delivering PRT. Extremely productive partnerships can be formed between parents and intervention providers. For example, in a home–school collaboration, we showed that when parents primed (previewed) academic exercises with their children in a relaxing, undemanding atmosphere, the children had far fewer behavior problems and much larger academic gains at school (L.K. Koegel, Koegel, Frea, & Green-Hopkins, 2003). Continuing to look at the effect of parent

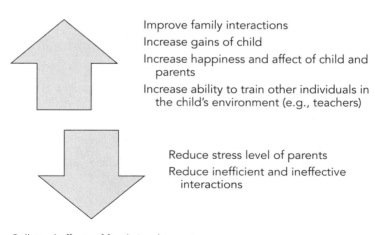

Improve family interactions
Increase gains of child
Increase happiness and affect of child and parents
Increase ability to train other individuals in the child's environment (e.g., teachers)

Reduce stress level of parents
Reduce inefficient and ineffective interactions

Collateral effects of family involvement.

partnerships with professionals, Brookman-Frazee (2004) examined the difference between situations in which the trainer took a directive role and those in which the trainer took a collaborative role, asking for the parent's input in implementation of intervention. As you may have guessed, although the children did learn new skills with both approaches, the parents were far happier in the collaborative model than in the directive model. Similarly, we looked at whether social skills would improve if the parents arranged playdates based upon suggestions of potential friends made by the children's teachers. With this parent–professional collaboration, we found that there were dramatic gains in child social behavior under such conditions, with strong peer friendships eventually forming (R.L. Koegel, Werner, Vismara, & Koegel, 2005).

Parents as a key component in intervention.

Overall, the literature clearly shows that incorporating parents as an integral and active part of the intervention is productive for child improvement and for the quality of life for the entire family. Thus, parent involvement in PRT is not a luxury; it is a key component of any successful treatment.

Myth: Children with autism need to learn from a professional. Parents often interfere in the learning process.

Reality: If parents do not learn how to implement the intervention procedures, their children will learn more slowly and will have difficulties generalizing and maintaining their gains.

MAKING IT WORK IN EVERYDAY SETTINGS

Near Santa Barbara, there is an especially nice destination with a pleasant little lake. Not long ago, a family decided to spend the day there. As the family admired the lake, one of the children fell into the water. Tragically, he didn't know how to swim. Faster than lightning, the father jumped in after him and threw the small child to terrified people anxiously waiting by the shore. They quickly pulled the small child to safety, but in the meantime the father disappeared below the water. Later, police reported that the father didn't know how to swim, either, and drowned. It's such a sad story, but the reason we retell it is to exemplify parents' commitment to their children. When his son fell into the water, this father didn't stop and ponder. He didn't think to himself, "If I jump in, I may drown, because I don't know how to swim." He didn't give it a second thought. When he saw his child in trouble, he immediately jumped in to save the child's life.

Parents of children with autism have this same powerful love for their children. They will do anything to help their children. If something is not right, they don't stop and ponder, as if it were an academic issue; they take action. Whether it be getting their child in the best educational setting or working for hours with their child, their commitment is unwavering. Parents' commitment is so helpful for children on the spectrum. Using this parental energy is tremendously necessary and useful for parent education, because parents can provide constant learning opportunities for their child throughout the day.

So how do parents get involved with the intervention in everyday settings? If you are a parent, make sure that you are a part of your child's intervention sessions. If you are a teacher or therapist, make sure that your student's parents are actively—very actively—involved. If possible, watch parents work with their child and provide them with feedback. Tell them what they are doing correctly, and give gentle guidance to change the things that may be less helpful for their child or to alert them to areas where they may inadvertently be causing or maintaining behavior problems. If you are a parent, ask if you can work with your child in a professional's presence and get feedback. We call this "practice with feedback," and many competent professionals will be able to provide you with this service. This practice will give you an idea of how you're doing and what areas need improvement.

Examples of Ways Parents Can Get Involved

- Get notes home from school.
- Have therapists videotape sessions.
- Observe the child during a lunch break.
- Work on socialization after school.
- Schedule monthly team meetings.

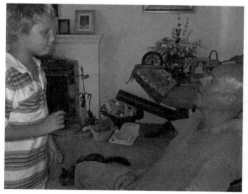

Here a child and his father are having fun playing a game of making faces that show different emotions. The child is learning, and both the child and his father are enjoying themselves in a very meaningful and happy way.

Whether it is speech therapy, behavior intervention, or academics, the child will learn faster and maintain learned behaviors longer if her parents are able to help her practice at home, in community settings, after school, over the weekend, and on family vacations. If you are a working parent, make sure you get notes from school and other activities that clearly describe what is being worked on in a step-by-step manner and how you can follow through. If possible, ask teachers and other therapists to videotape sessions for you, and any time you have a day off or a lunch break, go observe your child. And don't forget socialization. Parents can work on socialization after school and during the weekend. Ask your child's teacher or aide about another child who gets along well with your child, and then arrange a playdate or have the children meet for ice cream after school.

Make sure you schedule monthly meetings with the whole team. You can write regular coordination meetings into the child's individualized education program (IEP) if you want to make sure they happen. Regular meetings are often essential to making sure everyone is coordinating on goals and using the same intervention techniques. And if you, as a parent, want to show your appreciation, have your child help you bake a batch of cookies to bring to the team meeting. If your work hours make it difficult to meet, try to meet during lunch or at least have a monthly phone call with your child's teacher. Family involvement makes a huge difference. Be there and be an active part.

The Smith family had the financial resources to hire the best therapists money could buy. They used a wing of their home and had therapists work with their child, David, for 80 hours a week. The therapists went to school with him and spent the rest of the afternoon and evening working with him. Unfortunately, weekends were a disaster. Outside the structure of school or therapy sessions, David turned into a little monster. He was disruptive at the slightest demand and ran around constantly. The Smiths asked for help, and we provided them with parent education, starting with how to motivate David to perform activities (see Chapter 2) and how to follow through once they had given him an instruction. David's parents worked with him in a variety of community settings, and a parent educator accompanied them on these outings to provide support and feedback on their approach and just to guide them if they needed to ignore inappropriate or disruptive behaviors. David gradually improved, and after about four months of twice-weekly parent education sessions, the family was able to go on many outings such as trips to the grocery store and even a fast-food restaurant. They even learned how to have David clean up his toys and get ready for bed all by himself. The quality of their entire family life changed. Family involvement made a huge difference, making life easier for everyone, and it was something money couldn't buy.

Ask Yourself

PARENTS

1. Do I know all my child's goals?
2. Do I know how to work with my child to move toward these goals?
3. Am I keeping in touch with my child's teachers and therapists so that my child's program is coordinated, so that I know my child's friends, and so that I know exactly how everyone is working with him or her?

TEACHERS

1. Do I regularly coordinate with parents on goals and treatment procedures?
2. Am I working on goals that are important to my student's family?
3. Is everyone on the "team" using a consistent teaching approach?

6

How to
Minimize Parent Stress

Daniel is in elementary school. He is doing well, but he has occasional aggressive incidents and is often sent home from school. He has a loving family that cares about him immensely, but his mother is overcome with stress. She constantly worries that the school will call (again) saying that he needs to be taken home because of bad behavior, that he will do something embarrassing in public, or that other people won't treat him well. Sometimes she worries so much that it exhausts her.

Daniel's mother isn't alone. There is no doubt that the parents of children on the spectrum experience a significant amount of stress that just doesn't seem to go away. We've worked for a long, long time on helping parents reduce their stress, but this area has been challenging and, for many parents, elusive. However, some things do seem to help, such as keeping a journal, getting time away from the kids (as long as a trustworthy baby sitter is available), and surrounding the family with people who are willing to help. But even then, it seems that such things only reduce the stress; they don't completely eliminate it. We have also learned that parent education programs can either increase or reduce stress. Specifically, if parent education programs are conducted in a way that requires parents to take time out of their busy schedules to sit down and work with their child, stress levels increase. Parents are busy. They have jobs, chores, other children, and so forth. If they don't get a chance to sit down

and work on assignments that were given in parent education programs, they feel guilty and their stress increases.
It's kind of like going to a mechanic when your car is bro-
ken and having the mechanic say, "How about if I teach you
how to fix your car? That way, you'll be able to fix it any
time it acts up again." Too much! Most of us would probably feel overwhelmed at the thought of taking time out of
our busy schedules to fix our own car. We'd much rather
just drop it off and have a competent mechanic do the work.
However, we are willing to do the day-to-day things, such
as getting gas, filling the tires, and checking the oil, that
keep it running. It's the same with parents—they need to be
actively implementing the intervention but not in a way that
increases their stress.

The importance of this issue can't be underestimated.
If parents are taught how to implement goals within the
context of their everyday routines, stress levels decrease.

Stress is greatly reduced when Pivotal Response Treatment
is implemented. This results in measurable improvements in
affect for the whole family.

Further, having parents participate in selecting goals (see Chapter 1) and teaching them to implement intervention within the context of their everyday routines in natural settings can have the combined effect of speeding up their child's learning curve and reducing parental stress. Not by coincidence, this parental use of naturalistic intervention also gives way to higher levels of overall parent enthusiasm, interest, and happiness (Schreibman et al., 1991).

Another way to reduce stress is participating in a parent support group. It is important that this group be carefully planned: Only a few types of support groups actually work. Most end up being discontinued (see Albanese, San Miguel, & Koegel, 1995). Parents report that if they get together with other parents who "complain" about how difficult things are and how incompetent school personnel are, stress increases. However, if the group sessions are conducted by an experienced professional who guides the discussion to focus on problem solving, stress can be reduced, and parents report that they enjoy the group.

Teachers and interventionists can help by listening and rejoicing in the little accomplishments of the child, no matter how small. Parents who are under significant levels of stress need to know that even their child's little accomplishments are important. Parents need support when they parent correctly—it helps when teachers or interventionists remember to compliment them regularly on their successes. And if a child has a problem, teachers and therapists can suggest ideas they have read in the literature that may help. There is nothing worse for a parent than a teacher or interventionist who constantly points out the negatives. It is important for teachers and therapists to be part of the solution, not part of the problem.

No doubt, further research is essential to determine the best ways that teachers, interventionists, family members, and society in general can help the parents of children with

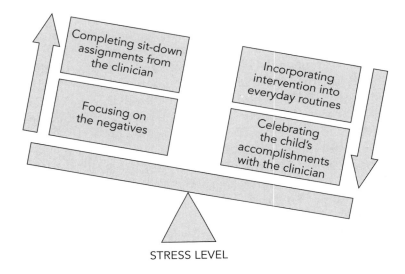

STRESS LEVEL

Reducing parental stress.

autism spectrum disorders decrease their stress. But we've begun the process by determining that this is a problem area. To be sure, this is not an exhaustive list of suggestions but just a start on ideas that should help decrease stress. However, more research is necessary to figure out ways to not just reduce parental stress, but to get it within typical limits. And not to decrease it temporarily, but permanently. This is our obligation as a society to each and every parent of a child with autism.

THE RESEARCH TO BACK IT: PARENT STRESS

Our research on parental stress unambiguously documents that there is an unbelievable amount of stress associated with having a child with autism (R.L. Koegel, Schreibman, et al., 1992). And there are specific patterns and types of stress that are common among all parents of children with autism (as measured on the Questionnaire on Resources and Stress for Families with Chronically Ill or Handicapped Members, Holroyd, 1987). That is, parents of children with autism are very different from parents of typically developing children with regard to their stress relating to dependency and management, cognitive impairment, limits on family opportunity, and life-span care. This isn't surprising. Parents have to manage more behaviors, the children's language difficulties make them more dependent and interfere with cognitive functioning, and parents worry about life over the long haul. It adds up to high stress. Interestingly, the types of stress are similar across mothers who live in different cultural and geographic environments and who have children of different ages and different levels of functioning (R.L. Koegel, Schreibman, et al., 1992). Fathers feel stress too but in different areas (Moes, Koegel, Schreibman, & Loos, 1992). We compared data on mothers and fathers using three different tests: the Questionnaire on Resources and Stress, the Coping Health Inventory for Parents (CHIP; McCubbin, McCubbin, Nevin, & Cauble, 1981), and the Beck Depression Inventory (Beck & Steer, 1987). Although the mothers showed significantly more stress than fathers, the patterns seemed to be related to societal roles. That is, mothers were most stressed in areas relating to child care and nurturing their children, and fathers were most stressed by financial concerns related to their ability to secure intervention for their children. For the families that participated in the study, fathers were the primary source of income for families, and mothers were the primary child care providers. As these traditional parenting roles change, it may be that the types of stress families experience may also change.

An interesting finding is that it doesn't seem as though parental stress necessarily goes away with parent education. You might think that once parents have a set of skills to handle their children's behaviors and teach new skills,

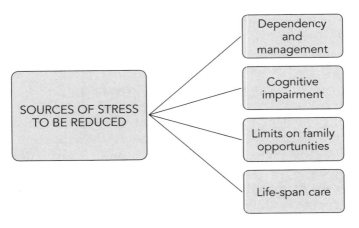

Sources of parental stress.

they'd have low stress. But no. Even if they had participated in parent education programs and had excellent control over their child's behavior, it didn't necessarily decrease stress (R.L. Koegel et al., 1996). Also, parents really worry about their child's cognitive abilities. Even if the child is bright, parents feel that traditional academic testing may place the child in the cognitively impaired range, especially because most standardized testing relies heavily on communication—a primary challenge area for children with autism. In addition, many children on the spectrum have behavior problems, so it is difficult to take them into public places. Thus, families can engage in a limited number of activities. Also, many parents are completely stressed about the negative reactions they experience from the community. In short, parents are really worried and stressed out about their children, and this just doesn't seem to go away. They feel that their child's dependency would require someone with their level of experience and their level of devotion, and they are aware that they are likely to die before their child; thus, they are unequivocally stressed about whether the child will always continue to receive the love and devotion that they have provided.

Our findings related to stress are completely consistent with other studies in this field (e.g., Bouma & Schweitzer, 1990; Bristol & Schopler, 1983; Holroyd & McArthur, 1976) and exemplify the importance of developing intervention programs and community supports that reduce stress.

One area that may receive attention in the future relates to cultural variables that may create or reduce stress in parents of children with autism. For example, research in the area of cultural diversity suggests that where there is broad extended family support for child rearing (e.g., lots of relatives to help out with the child and to provide support), stresses related to caring for children are much lower than in cultures in which families raise their children more independently and relatives live far away. Continued research in such areas is likely to be extremely important for the field of autism, since offers of social support, though helpful for most families, can also be perceived as stressful if they are incompatible with a family's views or values (Bernheimer, Gallimore, & Weisner, 1990; Gallimore, Weisner, Kaufman, & Bernheimer, 1989). Other stresses unrelated to the family may create even more issues for parents of children with autism, leading to difficulty working with their child and participating in parent education programs. For example, stressful personal circumstances, such as health problems, loss of a job, or marital discord, may make implementing the myriad of intervention procedures with a child with autism extremely difficult (Plienis, Robbins, & Dunlap, 1988).

Overall, there's an essential need to develop interventions that not only help the child with autism improve but also consider the impact on the entire family. Understanding where particular areas of stress are can guide us toward developing more effective programs, whether it be dealing first with stressful personal circumstances or helping to plan for long-term care to ensure a child's needs will be met effectively and with care and devotion. For example, it is important to realize that certain types of interventions may improve child behavior but may also increase parental stress, while other types of interventions may both improve the child's behavior and simultaneously reduce parental stress. PRT has been particularly effective in this regard, improving family interactions in general while reducing the stress of those interactions (R.L. Koegel et al., 1996).

Myth: Parents should not be expected to work with their children. It causes them increased stress and anxiety.

Reality: Teaching parents to implement the intervention within the context of their everyday routines can reduce parental stress (see Chapters 1 and 2).

MAKING IT WORK IN EVERYDAY SETTINGS

Everyone deals with stress differently, and different things reduce stress for different people. If you are a parent of a child with autism, you almost certainly are experiencing stress, so it's a good exercise to take a moment to make a list of activities that make you feel good and relax you (Barry & Singer, 2002). From our experience, it also seems to help if you make a list of activities that make you feel better in the morning. Is it that quiet cup of coffee with a good book or a jog in the park? Then, make time to do those things. In our clinical experience, we have noted other things that may help as well. If your child's morning routine is driving you nuts, you may wish to make it a priority to teach your child to be more independent in that area, whether it be setting an alarm clock and getting up on his own so that you have a few extra minutes of rest, or teaching her to pack her own lunch so that you have one less chore to do. What about the rest of the time? Does it relax you to take some time to be by yourself or with your significant other?

On the flip side, if you're feeling overwhelmed with homework and teaching activities, ask your child's teacher or therapist to help you find ways to work on those behaviors within your everyday routines. For example, your child can learn math while cooking, and that's a lot more practical than sitting at a desk doing worksheets. Reading a recipe is a great way to practice phonics and math, and your child might just help you out when you're preparing dinner. Your child will eventually need to learn how to clean, cook, and take care of himself, and the sooner you teach him, the easier your life will be. Although we have not systematically studied all of these techniques yet, overall, we have found that teaching in the context of natural activities reduces stress (R.L. Koegel et al., 1996).

Now think about the people in your life. Do they support you or cause you more stress? If you're not feeling relaxed when you are with other people, figure out what needs to change. Can you ask your mother-in-law to take your child for a few hours instead of visiting your home? Can you ask your child's teacher to think of three ways in which she could keep him at school and work on decreasing behavior problems, rather than calling you to pick him up each time? Take the time to figure out what is causing you stress and work to decrease those causes. And at the same time, figure out what makes you less stressed and work toward increasing those activities. You'll be a better (and happier) parent if you do.

If you are a teacher or interventionist, in addition to helping the parents of your students learn how to implement the intervention in their everyday settings, go that extra mile to help the family of your student. Offer to keep the child after school for a few hours, take her for an outing once in a while, or just make a phone call to ask how the family is doing. If you can't do this, make sure to pick up the phone or send an e-mail about a success your student had. Relatedly, it is important to focus on strengths the child exhibits (Steiner, 2011). If the child is nonverbal, instead of saying that the child can't talk and needs to learn to talk, say something like, "Your child seems to be able to make a lot of 't' sounds so let's work on words that have the letter 't' in them." Also, ask the family if there are any goals that would make their lives easier, such as teaching the child to do homework independently, set the table, pack his own lunch, cook, clean, help out with the household chores, or feed the dog. And think about little things, such as having your student make a special holiday card for mom or dad. When parents are stressed, having that extra positive support can really make a difference.

Steps to Reduce Parental Stress

- Make a list of relaxing activities.
- Ask your child's teacher or therapist for help on challenging behaviors.
- Incorporate teaching into everyday activities.
- Surround yourself with supportive people.
- Focus on your child's strengths rather than deficits.

The Moras were a combined family. The mother had been married previously and had two teenage children from her first marriage and two preschool children from her second, the youngest of which was a daughter with autism. On top of that, they had a puppy and two cats. The father worked long hours, while mom stayed home. The stress of four children, including one with autism, was taking a toll on the parents' relationship. They rarely spent time together, and when they did, they argued constantly. Both were exhausted—dad from working so hard and mom from parenting without any help from her husband. They told us that they had many fond memories of the wonderful, romantic things they had done together in the past, but those activities were now nonexistent.

After careful contemplation about what might help the family, we realized that a few things were keeping them from spending time together. First, mom was extremely worried about leaving her youngest daughter with a baby sitter. Because her daughter had communication delays and behavior problems, she worried that the neighborhood baby sitter wouldn't have the skills to work with the child and that if something went wrong, her daughter wouldn't be able to tell her. What we did was to have one of our highly skilled therapists go to their home one evening a week so that the parents could have a date night. Mom could fully relax when she went out, knowing that her child was in good, skilled hands. We had some other ideas, too. We helped organize things around the house and changed the household routines by having the children clean up their toys and their dishes from dinner and pack lunches for the next day, so the house was clean and there wasn't a lot of work to do after the parents' date nights. We also worked with dad to make sure the night out was special—really special. We helped him plan the date night in advance—to make reservations at a nice restaurant and buy movie tickets. He even started bringing his wife flowers. In addition, while we were at the home, we began working with the family's teenage son to teach him some of the techniques for working with his youngest sister.

Gradually, we noticed that the father began taking more of a role in planning dates, without our prompts, and over time he began spending more time at home. He had been working long hours partly because he was reluctant to come home when fighting seemed inevitable. The marriage started improving. Eventually, he asked his wife to spend a few hours a day assisting at his office while the children were at school. The mother greatly enjoyed this time and used some of her earnings to hire a housekeeper to clean their home once a week—a task she hated. Some families may need more than a date night once a week to reduce their stress, but in this case, working with the family system (including the older brother), improving the organization of the house, and simply providing an opportunity for the parents to have fun together were the keys to improving this couple's marriage and the family's life.

Ask Yourself

PARENTS

1. What makes me feel stressed out, and how can I change that?
2. What are the activities that make me happy, and how can I increase these activities?
3. What chores can I teach my child that will make my life easier?

TEACHERS

1. What am I doing to help decrease the stress of my student's parents?
2. Am I teaching the parents of my student how to work on target goals within the context of everyday activities?
3. Have I included goals into the curriculum that will ease parental stress at home?

7

Treatment and Assessment in Natural Environments

I. TREATMENT IN NATURAL ENVIRONMENTS

Sarah was in a special education classroom in elementary school. The classroom was small, with only eight children with a combination of different disabilities, including two children with autism, five children with language delays, and one child with Down syndrome. Sarah's academic skills were uneven, with strengths in sight-reading and math and difficulties in reading comprehension and other language-based activities. Last year she was the only child with autism in her class, but this year they have added another child with autism and severe disruptive behavior. Sarah has begun picking up inappropriate behaviors from this other child. Her parents have asked the director of special education about including her in a general education classroom, but he says that first the special education staff needs to get the students "ready" to be in general education, and then they will consider moving her toward general education. Is this a good approach?

Sarah's parents were right to be concerned. It is *so* important to get students with autism included with typically developing children, and in typical settings, at as early an age as possible. Kids on the spectrum need to practice their social goals with their typically developing peers and need to learn how to model after their typically developing peers who already have good social skills. The "readiness" model isn't usually effective, and often children with disabilities fall even farther behind when they are segregated from their typically developing peers and are provided with a curriculum different from what is presented in the general education classroom. In short, whenever possible, teaching needs to be done in the natural environment. That means general education classes, after-school activities and classes, and family outings—just as if the child doesn't have a disability. Forget about the old days of clinical rooms, free from the distractions of toys and without pictures on the walls, where a small number of students, all with disabilities, worked on curricula that differed dramatically (usually being at a much lower level) from the curricula provided to typically developing children. That isn't the natural environment and isn't an ideal setting for teaching a child with autism. If you are a parent, please don't even consider emptying out your basement or that extra guest room so that your child can be sequestered in a distraction-free setting. If a child with autism is going to live, work, and have relationships in the "real world" as an adult, he needs to be taught from the beginning how to survive in all of the natural environments he would experience if he didn't have a disability. That's the way to give him the best chance for becoming fully included as an adult.

Working in these everyday settings solves the huge generalization problems we used to have in our clinics. To

be specific, we used to teach the kids in distraction-free environments. We minimized the number of pictures on the walls and in every way tried to make sure that there weren't any things around that would distract the children. Even though they did learn in those settings, the children had trouble us-
ing those newly learned behaviors
in their natural environments. We
call this a lack of generalization.
In other words, they had difficulties generalizing the use of new
behaviors to other environments, to
new tasks that weren't specifically
taught, and even to new people. For
example, a child may perform per-

> ### *Generalization*
> Applying learned behaviors
> • To other environments
> • To other behaviors
> • With other people
> • Over time for durability

fectly well on math problems on worksheets, but when she goes to the store and can't add up the prices of two items, all those math sheets were meaningless. Or if she can label a picture of a zebra but goes to the zoo and has no idea what the black-and-white-striped animal with four legs is, the teaching was pretty much useless from the perspective of life in the real world. So solving the generalization problem means, in part, teaching the child in general education classes whenever possible; taking her into everyday settings such as restaurants, the grocery store, or the toy store; having her participate in after-school clubs and activities; and so forth. The child with autism should be treated the same way as a child without a disability. In these natural settings, we don't need to worry about generalization issues, and the child with autism will learn to perform in the environments in which we expect her to participate as she grows. Treatment in the natural, everyday setting is critical for the most positive outcomes.

THE RESEARCH TO PROVE IT

In Chapter 5, we discussed how important family involvement is, but another important feature of PRT is that the intervention takes place in the natural environment. If you're a parent, this means that you'll want to make sure that your child is participating in whatever classroom, after-school program, leisure activity, or other setting you would choose if your child didn't have a disability. Tons of research is accumulating showing the many benefits of treatment in the natural environment.

Natural versus Specialized or Segregated Environments

Every single theory of child development is based on the assumptions that children will be reared in natural environments and that removing typically developing children from their natural environments will most likely cause some type of developmental harm. That is, children need to be exposed to natural stimuli in order to have natural development. However, historically, in the treatment of autism, this exposure to natural stimulation has not always been the case when people attempted to "help" children with disabilities. Only a few decades ago, most people with autism spent their lives in a locked mental hospital, and most doctors recommended this approach.

Although a few progressive individuals (who had excellent results), such as Jean Marc Gaspard Itard in the early 1800s and Helena Devereaux in the early 1900s, attempted to provide intensive and individualized intervention in natural settings by bringing individuals with disabilities into their homes, they were by far the exception to the rule. Their approach was quite a change from the usual treatment that had endured for many, many decades—all of which was conducted in a segregated setting involving only people with disabilities. It's important to remember that, at that time, very few scientifically sound interventions were available, and interventionists thought that such isolated settings would provide the opportunity for intensive therapy conducted 24 hours a day, 7 days a week. Unfortunately, the gains in those settings were not what people had hoped to see. Once children with autism were placed in an institutional setting, they tended to remain there for the rest of their lives. Though the lack of progress was bad enough, there were other concerns as well. The mental hospitals were very different from the children's natural communities. The hospitals were located in isolated areas. They were usually locked. In fact, they were often double and triple locked so the children couldn't escape. The children were confined to bedrooms and day areas, and they interacted only with other children who also had autism. The physical facilities tended to be in poor condition because they were continually exposed to extremely disruptive, often non–toilet-trained children. Mental hospitals are expensive to operate at the best of times, and few institutions had the desire or means to create a homelike environment that would be quickly destroyed by children who didn't seem to appreciate kind staff and nice toys. In the end, it was a vicious circle.

Observational Learning

- Absence of good role models may cause children with autism to learn in atypical ways.
- Children with autism can gain appropriate behaviors through observing typically developing peers.

To make matters worse, the primary intervention for changing behavior was punishment. The children were frequently restrained, and it was common to witness staff regularly attempting to control the children's problem behaviors with severe physical punishment, such as a high-voltage electric shock. Such living conditions were bad in themselves, but they were also ineffective for producing positive treatment outcomes. For example, Lovaas et al. (1973) showed that, in the hospital setting, very expensive and time-consuming treatments were necessary to make changes in the children's behavior and, even with the best treatments, the children's gains did not continue when they were discharged from the hospital.

A number of subsequent studies showed that in addition to the hospital setting being a problem, the artificial nature of the intervention tasks was also problematic. That is, when treatment involves using artificial stimuli such as flashcards in a drill-practice format, the resulting improvements in child response and in family interactions, as a whole, are inferior to when the intervention is conducted within natural contexts. In fact, the same is true for most behaviors. Children with autism more effectively learn even behaviors that are traditionally taught in isolated contexts, such as articulation, if they are taught under more naturalistic conditions. In our research, we showed that the intelligibility of children's speech could be improved far more efficiently when intervention was conducted within a natural context (L.K. Koegel et al., 1998). As an illustration, if a child was having difficulty learning how to produce the letter *f*, the study showed that intelligible speech would be learned more efficiently if the children were asked to request favorite items beginning with the letter *f* instead of asking them to name flashcards with pictures of items beginning with the letter *f*. For example, one little guy we worked with loved to play with balls. So, with that in mind, we gathered together a whole bunch of balls and named them with words that began with the letter *f*, such as a "football," a "funny" ball, a "foam" ball, and so forth. He was given these balls to play with when he requested them with a correct production of the letter *f* in the word. Using these fun activities in natural contexts proved more effective than using flashcards. Furthermore, the children were much less disruptive. Thus, the teacher was able to devote far more time to teaching and did not need to spend much, if any, time working on reducing disruptive behavior. We also found that when we were working with the flashcards, the children had difficulty generalizing the new sound outside of the speech therapy session; when we used the balls, the children generalized the sounds easily.

Child behavior improves more when intervention is conducted in a naturalistic context. However, it is interesting to note that a number of studies also showed that family interactions improve as well when intervention is conducted in a naturalistic context. As previously mentioned, Schreibman et al. (1991) and R.L. Koegel et al. (1996) showed that family interactions are happier and less stressful when intervention is conducted within the naturalistic context.

Another reason natural settings are important relates to observational learning. Researchers have shown that the absence of good role models may cause children with autism to learn in atypical ways (Varni, Lovaas, Koegel, & Everett, 1979). With minimal effort, children with autism can learn new tasks by observing typically developing individuals around them (Egel, Richman, & Koegel, 1981). These findings stress the importance of the treatment context. That is, observational learning may be different if the child's environment is composed of only children with autism versus a context that is composed primarily of typically developing children. When a child's primary peer role models have delayed communication, disruptive behaviors, and limited interests, it is quite difficult, if not impossible, for her to acquire typical behaviors through observation. In contrast, when her peers are typically developing children, the child can observe and gain a lot of typical behavior. This idea is

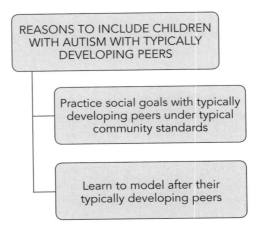

Importance of inclusion.

consistent with theories of child development (cf. Bijou & Baer, 1966; Bandura, 1969).

Another benefit relates to generalization. Years ago we showed, in several studies, that teaching children with autism in a segregated, one-to-one format produced almost no generalization—not even to a small-group context (R.L. Koegel & Rincover, 1974; Russo & Koegel, 1977). We also showed that even after children had participated in extensive one-to-one teaching, they still required special intervention to be successful in a general education classroom. The bottom line is that teaching in a very specialized, segregated environment, whether it produces gains in that environment, is not likely to produce the type of gains that will be helpful in nonsegregated environments. Thus, there is no doubt that the literature strongly supports inclusive settings for the benefit of all children—with and without disabilities.

Another important issue is that many people erroneously believe that human contact is aversive to children with autism and that it is better to set up an artificial environment with limited human interactions. In fact, people used to

Pivotal Response Treatment encourages participation and treatment in natural environments. These children enjoy the beach, and the activity provides opportunities to teach many skills in an enjoyable manner.

think that children with autism did better in settings that were free from distractions. However, when this question was studied systematically, it turned out that those types of "special environments" were not helpful. We found that the children actually had more trouble learning certain tasks in those types of settings and benefited from the help of adults and peers (cf. Russo, Koegel, & Lovaas, 1978). In fact, human contact seems to be very comforting and helpful to a child with autism—another reason for teaching in natural contexts.

Naturalistic Contexts for Assessment

Having seen the difference the environment can make for teaching, think about what might happen when standardized assessments are conducted in artificial environments and whether such testing will yield useful information for suggesting treatment. A growing body of evidence suggests that standardized tests yield different information than naturalistic assessments (Condouris, Meyer, & Tager-Flusberg,

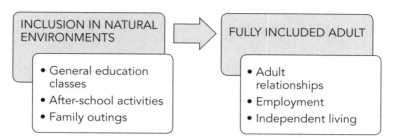

How inclusion during childhood has an impact on adulthood.

2003; Dawson, Soulières, Gernsbacher, & Mottron, 2007; Dunn, Flax, Sliwinski, & Aram, 1996; Edelson, 2005). For example, we showed that for children with autism who exhibit behavior problems, assessments of vocabulary, language, and intelligence quotients are highly variable depending on the children's level of motivation (L.K. Koegel, Koegel, & Smith, 1997). Specifically, when a psychologist, speech and language specialist, teacher, or other examiner administers a test under strictly standardized conditions, without providing any specific motivational component such as those included in PRT, the children will score very poorly on the test. In fact, the results may suggest that the children have severe cognitive impairments and severely delayed language. However, when motivational components are included, the same children will show dramatically higher levels of performance, with test results sometimes showing functioning in the average range. Thus, standardized tests can grossly underestimate the abilities of a child with autism. It appears that the artificial context is measuring the children's lack of motivation to perform rather than measuring their abilities (Kuriakose & Koegel, 2010). This point is key because testing is important for developing goals. If the test underestimates a child's ability, the child may spend a whole year—or longer—being taught target behaviors that are already well known, making school virtually useless.

Procedures for Teaching in Natural Environments

We know that intervention in natural environments produces large and meaningful gains for children with autism. Yet, some may wonder if it is really feasible to conduct intensive specialized intervention under such conditions. Interestingly, an abundance of research suggests that intervention in the natural environment is relatively simple to implement as well as extremely effective. Many years ago, when most children with autism were routinely excluded from general education settings, we showed that inclusion was possible, and there were many immediate gains (Russo & Koegel, 1977). Although it was necessary to provide training (brief and specialized) for the general education teachers in order for the interventions to be effective, there were huge gains with very little cost, and the social and educational benefits continued over the years (see also Harrower & Dunlap, 2001; Owen-DeSchryver, Carr, Cale, & Blakeley-Smith, 2008; Strain, McGee, & Kohler, 2001). Further, with only a small amount of training, teacher-implemented PRT in a general education classroom is simple to accomplish and highly successful in improving communication for children with autism (Smith & Camarata, 1999). In addition to teachers, with only a small amount of specialized training peers can also successfully implement PRT in natural contexts, yielding improvements in complex social behaviors (Pierce & Schreibman, 1995).

The studies just mentioned show that inclusion is relatively easy to accomplish, but the research is also very clear that merely placing children with autism in natural contexts, by itself, is not likely to produce benefits. Teacher training, peer training, and a coordination of the efforts of everyone involved are critical for the best outcomes. A lack of coordination can be especially problematic. For example, behavioral contrast might occur if two intervention provid-

Historical treatments versus Pivotal Response Treatment (PRT)

	Historical treatments	PRT
Location of intervention	Segregated environments Isolated mental hospitals	Natural environments Inclusion with typical peers
Primary intervention	Punishment/rewards Restraints	Positive behavior support Focus on motivation
Stimulus	Artificial stimulus Example: flashcards	Motivational stimulus Examples: toys, books
Generalization and maintenance	Difficulty generalizing and maintaining new behaviors to outside environments	Increase in generalization and maintenance of new behaviors to outside environments
Interaction	Human contact believed to be aversive to children with autism	Human contact believed to be comforting and beneficial to children with autism

ers implement intervention goals with slight differences in the teaching procedures (R.L. Koegel, Egel, & Williams, 1980). All interventionists have seen children who improve in one environment but deteriorate in another if the intervention is being implemented differently in each setting. In another study, we showed that toilet training was a complete failure when the procedures weren't coordinated and each intervention in each environment differed. However, after the intervention was coordinated across all of the children's environments, the children were very rapidly toilet trained (Dunlap, Koegel, & Kern, 1984). So successful was the coordination program that children often were toilet trained within a day or two, and even older children who were nonverbal were trained in all settings within 2 weeks.

Another effective strategy that gives individuals with autism a tool, in a sense, for providing their own intervention is self-management. This involves teaching the student to discriminate between an appropriate and an inappropriate behavior and then to independently monitor either the occurrence or the time interval of the appropriate behavior. Children with autism can learn to respond appropriately if the target behavior is programmed to occur through self-management (L.K. Koegel, Koegel, Hurley, & Frea, 1992). Children who are taught a self-management technique to reduce stereotypic behavior in one setting can then use the technique to produce the same gains in other settings, without the need of an interventionist in those additional settings (R.L. Koegel & Koegel, 1990). This generalization makes the intervention both efficient and cost effective.

In summary, the literature suggests that children with autism can be assessed and treated most effectively under natural conditions and that they benefit from interactions with typically developing children. Many procedures for implementing intervention in natural settings are so simple that even the children's peers can be taught to implement them effectively. There's no doubt: Natural settings produce the best outcomes. And there is no reason to fear doing natural interventions because of a naïve feeling that they would be too difficult or expensive to implement. They aren't.

Myth: It is better to teach children with autism in special, distraction-free environments or in classes for children with severe disabilities than to move them into mainstream settings.

Reality: Children with autism spectrum disorders learn better and have fewer problems transferring the use of their newly learned behaviors to other settings when teaching is implemented in everyday settings.

MAKING IT WORK IN EVERYDAY SETTINGS

If you are a parent, please, take your child everywhere with you. It may be difficult at first, but it is the best thing in the long run. If a shopping trip would be a total disaster, start out by just going to the store for one item—a favorite item, if possible—so the outing is set up to have a natural reward. Enroll your child in after-school activities and clubs—as many as you can. She may need an aide with her at first, but this assistance can be faded over time. Yet right from the start, the exposure to typically developing children will give her a chance to expand her interests and be around those children's activities. Also, try to get or keep your child with typically developing children at school for as much of the day as possible. Probably all day is best. There is plenty of evidence to support the fact that kids do better socially and academically if they are included with their typically developing peers. If the general education teacher says that your child will be a distraction to the typically developing children, know that there is no evidence to support this. In fact, from our experience, and from the reports of other professionals (J. Anderson, personal communication, circa 1992) typically developing children seem to do better when a child with disabilities is included in the classroom. Perhaps the teachers learn to individualize the instruction, to use more motivational strategies, or to deal with different learning styles more effectively—all of which can help all the students. Whatever the reason, your child is likely to do better in a general education setting. Typically developing children are a fantastic resource and can be a great help for a child with autism, both socially and academically.

However, including a child in a general education classroom without the right support is likely to be a disaster for both short- and long-term development. Make sure there is a positive behavior support plan. Make sure someone is doing the curricular modifications if your child needs them. Be certain that the school personnel who are working with your child are well trained and know the IEP goals. Be sure that you are priming, or practicing, the work at home before the assignments are presented in class (L.K. Koegel, Koegel, et al., 2003). And make sure that someone is monitoring your child's progress in every area, including interactions with typically developing peers. Also, make the effort to have classmates visit your home outside of school (R.L. Koegel et al., 2005). Ask your child's teacher which students seem to work well with your child. You can start with short, planned playdates and gradually increase the length of time and the number of activities as your child experiences success. Long playdates often turn into disasters, and then neither the peer nor the child with autism is excited about another one. Make sure your child is helping you with as many activities around the house as possible—cooking, cleaning, doing the gardening, and grooming and dressing himself. This will help him become independent.

If you are a teacher or administrator, do everything you can to keep children with autism included with their typically developing peers. Know that there is no evidence to suggest that either the children with autism or their typically developing peers will perform better if segregation occurs. Teach the students the behaviors they will need to survive in the real world. And always incorporate the typically developing peers. You'll need lots of different intervention programs that include both the child with autism and typically developing peers, and many programs should be implemented simultaneously if you want the best outcome for your student.

As a therapist, make sure your sessions include outings in everyday settings. Meet with families at the park or playground and help work on social interaction. Go to stores and teach the child how to order, how to pay, how to be po-

This photo shows how children who have been fully included in general education, summer camps, and other peer-related activities can learn appropriate social interaction skills and be valued members of their peer group.

lite to others in these settings, and so forth. All of this will help your student immensely in adulthood.

J C's family moved to Santa Barbara when he was in the first grade. He had been in general education as a preschooler, but because of asocial and challenging behaviors, he was gradually isolated from his peers and spent only recess and lunch in the proximity of typically developing kids. Even then, though he sat near them, he virtually never interacted with them. By the time we started working with him, he had developed an effective repertoire of avoidance behaviors so that he didn't have to interact at all, hardly had to engage in any academics, and scared off most of his peers. If adults approached him, he said rude things and went back to flapping his hands and engaging in other types of repetitive behaviors. If the teacher gave him an assignment, he almost always did something destructive, such as tearing it up or marking all over it with his pencil, so that completing it was virtually impossible. And if another child approached him, he had an escalating number of tricks—starting with making loud noises and working up to aggression if the noises didn't work—for getting the peer out of his personal space, which consequently became larger than any other child's personal area.

During his first-grade year, against the recommendation of his previous school personnel and private therapists, we fully included JC into a general education classroom. We didn't leave him alone, though. We also gave the teachers the support they needed to help the whole class have a successful educational experience. We provided specialized one-to-one support for him and training for his teachers. We started by making sure that he associated the people in his life with positive things, rather than fearing that others were only there to provide him with drill-practice academic exercises and equally difficult social activities. The adults restructured his math, reading, and writing activities and had positive outcomes. He got to add favorite toys and write things that he wanted to do at recess. The letters we taught him were always the beginning of words of favorite things we gave him. For recess and lunch, his parents provided us with favorite food items that he could share with his friends. We used charts and self-management programs, and we learned through experience that if we told him we would come back with a small, intrinsically related reward if he did a small bit of his classwork, he usually complied and did the work independently. He improved a lot during the year and was able to participate to some extent in the same activities as his typically developing peers. He was improving. More important, he was becoming accepted.

By his second year, his behavior problems had decreased considerably, and we began increasing the amount of schoolwork he engaged in through partial participation. We also focused on peer interactions. And through a variety of programs (i.e., priming, self-management, video modeling, rewards, recruiting his typically developing peers, arranging reinforcing types of interactions and clubs around his interest), his social interaction improved. He continued to show dramatic academic and social gains. After several years, although he is still somewhat behind the academic and social level of his peers, he is working on and keeping up with the same curriculum that they are, and he is advancing every day. He demonstrates appropriate behavior in school, goes on (and has) regular playdates, has performed in a school play, and exhibits no behavior problems. He fits in. He is liked. And he is advancing academically and socially.

A large part of JC's success is due to the fact that he has been fully included with plenty of support programs and has been surrounded by typically developing peers whose behavior we use as a goal, who provide desirable role models, and who enjoy interacting with him. Only in a fully inclusive setting could his positive outcomes be realized. Again, realize that throughout this educational program we have been focusing on pivotal areas of motivating JC to want to learn and to want to interact with his typically developing peers. By doing so, he has been exposed to a continual therapy program for a more typical development with every move he makes.

Ask Yourself

PARENTS

1. Is my child participating in community settings?
2. Is my child interacting with typically developing peers at school and outside school?
3. Am I teaching my child activities that will create independence in the real world? Or is my child being forced into an unmotivating, restricted placement because he or she is not learning the skills required to have a happy life in the real world?

4. Am I creating opportunities to motivate my child to want to interact academically and socially in the real world? Is his or her confidence improving, and does he or she feel natural and typical among his or her peers?

TEACHERS

1. Have I provided the parents with names of children with whom their child gets along?
2. Have I created programs that help my student actively interact with his or her typically developing peers?
3. Is my student interacting in typical settings and engaging in work similar to that of his or her typically developing peers?
4. Am I creating motivating educational experiences with intrinsic rewards that will help all of my students, both those with typical development and those with atypical development, want to learn and want to use their knowledge in their everyday lives?

II. ASSESSMENT IN NATURAL ENVIRONMENTS

Alyssa is an older elementary school student who scores poorly on tests and doesn't even seem to care about doing well on them. On the basis of her test scores in class and her standardized test scores, the school has recommended a curriculum that her parents believe is far below her academic ability. At home she rarely has a problem following directions and generally complies with even complex requests. She has a huge vocabulary but performs horribly on standardized vocabulary tests. The parents called our center for advice, as they have come to a gridlock with the school.

TESTING AND THE SCHOOL CURRICULUM

You've probably guessed what our advice was. Tests are often given to determine a child's functioning level and to develop the appropriate IEP, home goals, and curriculum. When we think of tests, we usually think of IQ (cognitive) tests or language tests. These types of tests have a standard set of procedures for how they are given. The child is usually seated at a table, and the examiner uses pictures as stimuli to assess the child's knowledge. The important point to remember here is that there are a variety of ways a child can be tested, and this point is especially important for kids with autism. Let us give you an example of why this is so important. We were once giving a standardized, receptive vocabulary test to a young child with autism using black-and-white drawings of various items. We asked the child to point to the drawing of a bed, and he pointed to the drawing of an oven. His dad, who was watching us give the test through a one-way window, grabbed his forehead, exasperated, and said, "Every night I ask my son to go to bed, and every night when I ask him to go to bed, he jumps into bed. Not once has he jumped into the oven!" Often you get different information when you give a standardized test than when you test in the "real world." Some kids do better in the real world, some do worse, and some do the same. But if a child does better or worse in the real world and a curriculum is developed on the basis of test scores, the curriculum may be totally inappropriate.

This was the case with Alyssa. The test scores were not accurately predicting her ability but rather testing her lack of motivation. Once we implemented some teacher-made tests that incorporated motivational components and provided some incentives for getting correct answers on the standardized tests, we were able to assess her true functioning and develop appropriate goals accordingly.

Just think, if a child like Alyssa had vocabulary items on her IEP that she already functionally knew, she could spend a lot of time engaged in useless activities. Don't forget, though, that the opposite can happen. Sometimes kids will respond correctly on a test but have no idea how to use the tested item functionally. It is so important that kids have the right curriculum. And to get it right, it is essential to know whether the child can use the tested words, grammatical structures, behaviors, and so forth in everyday settings.

One likely problem in testing is that most standardized tests are not the least bit interesting to children with autism. They may be boring, dull, or just plain meaningless. In such cases, the child may engage in any type of behavior possible to get out of the testing situation, ranging from aggression, disruption, and refusal to answer the test questions to lethargy and a lack of responsiveness during the tests. Again, this is why we want to stress the need for natural environments for assessment. As in the examples above, a

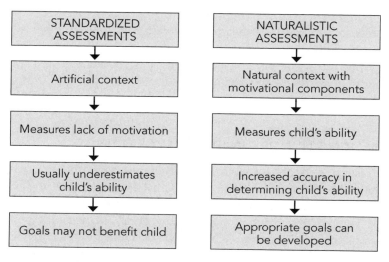

Standardized versus naturalistic assessments.

child may respond incorrectly to a test question but have absolutely no problem engaging in the appropriate behavior in the real world. Or, if the task is meaningful, such as dividing up a candy bar for the kids in the family, fractions may be easy, whereas a worksheet full of fractions may be utterly meaningless. Likewise, a child may be creating wonderful sentences that are grammatically correct, but if she is wandering around the playground throughout the recess and lunch periods and not talking with peers, the sentences are meaningless. The bottom line is this: In addition to intervention, assessments also need to be carried out in the child's everyday environments.

Myth: On-task behavior is more important than the level of curriculum. In other words, it's better to have a child engaged in easy academic activities or taught in an isolated setting than to have the child exhibit disruptive behavior.

Reality: Many children with autism spectrum disorders are provided with a curriculum that is far below their academic ability because they engage in disruptive behavior during boring, artificial testing tasks. They should receive a more appropriate curriculum.

MAKING IT WORK IN EVERYDAY SETTINGS

Assessments are important, but *valid* assessments are critical. The foundation of getting a valid assessment is understanding how the child functions in natural environments. If you are the teacher, observe the child in everyday settings, collect language samples to see what he is saying to his peers, watch his behavior, go to his home and see how he functions in everyday routines, and talk to his parents. If you are the parent, invite the school staff to see what areas are challenging and what strengths your child exhibits. If it's difficult for the school staff to go to your home, record your child on video and bring the recordings in to the IEP or parent–teacher conference. It's important to have practical and appropriate goals and curricula, and observations in natural settings will help you achieve this objective.

The next consideration is formal testing. We know that kids on the spectrum (and, in general, all people) tend to have more difficulty with tasks that aren't rewarding or aren't interesting. In contrast, if the task is meaningful and relevant, they are likely to do well. It all boils down to motivation. Thus, the first thing to think about is how the child performs in testing situations. Does he have difficulty with unfamiliar adults? Does he perform poorly when the task isn't meaningful? Does he have trouble with black-and-white drawings or the type of testing stimuli that were presented in the test? Your job is to make sure that the tests accurately reflect a child's ability and *not* his motivation or level of avoidance and disruptive behavior. If you think the tests are underestimating a child's ability, make sure that he is assessed under different conditions—that aren't necessarily standardized. This could be done by testing at the child's home, by using nonstandardized procedures, or through behavioral observations. If you are the tester, you must make sure that you have a valid indication of the abilities of the child. Invite the parents in to help with disruptive behavior or to help you understand what motivates the child.

Accurate evaluations lead to the right level of curriculum and target goals that will help the child move forward. This is essential for the long run. We know that students often use disruptive behavior to completely alter the teacher's curriculum. That is, most teachers keep making tasks easier and easier when the child becomes disruptive, instead of thinking about ways to decrease the disruptive behaviors and ways to make the curriculum more interesting. Eventually, schoolwork is completely below the child's academic ability, and the child is merely sitting in the classroom, engaging in meaningless tasks, and not learning anything. All because of the disruptive behavior. Don't be fooled by the child who uses other types of behavior, such as spacing out, lethargy, or unresponsiveness, to avoid classwork. This can be just as problematic, although it is often overlooked because it isn't disrupting the class. Remember, the child needs to progress and be challenged academically, just as typically developing children progress and are challenged.

So let's talk about ways that testing can be done more accurately. Here are a few practical ideas for testers:

- Find out what motivates the child and use that information in the testing situation. You could break up the test into small parts, use a reward as a motivator, or use any other strategy that motivates the child to respond.

- Interview the family so that you can be sure that the child is performing to her full capacity. For example, if the parents indicate that their child has a huge vocabulary but she is testing low, find out why.

- Make sure the child is tuned in and paying attention to your directions. Have him repeat the instruction before he responds or have him point to the testing items.

- Observe the child in natural settings to see how she functions in real-life situations.

- Give the child more breaks to engage in favorite activities during the testing situation.

- Let the child know exactly how many questions he will need to complete, so he doesn't view the tests as endless, monotonous tasks.

- Create your own tests that have more practical and meaningful questions.

Once again, getting the right testing, the right program, and the right curriculum will help children with autism reach their full potential.

W e observed this scenario during a school visit. One of the children, who exhibited a considerable amount of disruptive behavior, was participating in a completely different curriculum from the rest of the class. It was clear what was happening. Every time the child was given an assignment that was the least bit challenging, she began to engage in disruptive

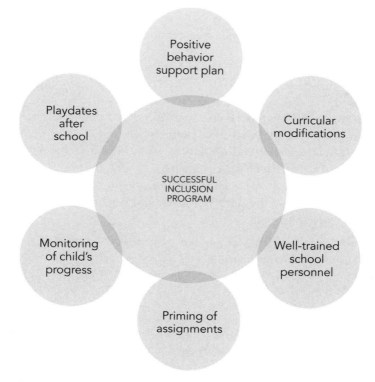

Components of a successful inclusion program.

behavior. When the assignments were easy—really easy and far below her ability—she worked away like a little angel. Although it was nice for her teacher and one-to-one aide when she was working quietly and independently, the child wasn't learning anything. In fact, the child had completely manipulated the teacher and the special education staff into developing a curriculum that was not challenging in the least. To make matters worse, the special education teacher, who was supposed to be including her, truly and honestly believed that having her student work independently was far more important than having her learn new things. After some discussion, we were able to begin interspersing more challenging tasks into the intervention. After a few months, she was able to participate in the same academic assignments as her peers, with only some minor modifications.

Sean was a bright high school student diagnosed with Asperger syndrome. He studied hard, could memorize just about anything, and was one of those kids who spent so much time reading that he was an expert on most topics, ranging from golf to world history. The problem was that his test performance was poor. He was getting Bs when he should have been getting As. For a high school student, grades mean everything in terms of getting into a good college. It seemed as though the knowledge wasn't the problem; it was the test. So here was the plan, sent in an e-mail:

> In regard to the tests, you may want to have all of his teachers start him on a self-management program for checking over his work. Simply have him check over each test question before turning in his test. To make sure he has done this, he should place a check mark next to the problem after he rechecks his work. If he turns in a test without the check mark by each problem, the teachers can ask him to go back to his desk and recheck his work. This should give him a helpful lifelong skill. Getting the top grades in high school will help him get into college, and I am sure he can do this, especially given that his grades are so high, even with the carelessness. Now, this is assuming that he has extra time at the end of the tests. If he doesn't, you may want

to consider getting an accommodation of extra time on the tests. He should qualify, especially if he isn't able to accurately perform due to time constraints.

The teachers were "onboard," and his parents told him the plan. The next week he scored As on all of his tests. He told his parents that as a high school student it would be really embarrassing if his teachers sent him back to his desk with his test, so he took it upon himself to check over every problem.

Ask Yourself

PARENTS

1. Has my child been accurately assessed?
2. Is my child benefiting from the curriculum?
3. Have accommodations been made in a way that makes the schoolwork challenging *and* motivating?

TEACHERS

1. Did I test the child in multiple environments and in a way that is motivating, so that I know the curriculum is appropriate?
2. Did I develop a challenging curriculum so that the child is learning?
3. Am I regularly asking myself whether I am presenting a less challenging curriculum when the child exhibits disruptive behavior?

8

Making Data Collection Easy in PRT

with Sarah Kuriakose

Many teachers, clinicians, and parents cringe when they hear the word "data." Collecting data can seem like an overwhelming task that interferes with natural PRT interactions. But data collection, which can be fun and productive when done well, is at the heart of effective intervention for many reasons. First, as a teacher or clinician, if you are starting a program, you need to monitor your student's progress just in case the program needs tweaking. Second, you need to monitor whether the child is reaching the goals you have developed. Finally, you want to assess how often and in what settings your student is using newly learned behaviors. Progress, acquisition, generalization, and maintenance are all important reasons for setting up a system to collect data. All children are different, and techniques that work quickly and dramatically for one child may need tweaking for another child. That's why you need data.

Research shows that data collection will also make a difference for your student. Yes, there are actually data about

Sarah Kuriakose, M.A., is completing her doctoral training in the Counseling, Clinical, and School Psychology Department at the University of California, Santa Barbara (with an anticipated completion date of June 2012). She is currently completing her predoctoral internship at Harvard Medical School in Boston, Massachusetts. She is the author of numerous publications in the field of autism spectrum disorders.

data collection! It turns out that teachers who frequently take data to monitor progress make more accurate decisions about children's curricula, and the students actually learn faster (Safer & Fleischman, 2005). One study conducted in special day classes found that children with teachers who systematically monitor student progress achieve 0.7 standard deviation units higher than children whose progress is not monitored (Fuchs & Fuchs, 1986). The bottom line is that, when implementing an intervention program, you must systematically collect data to ensure effectiveness, and data need to be collected in an easily feasible manner at various points in time—before intervention begins, during intervention, and after intervention is finished. Additionally, you'll want to collect generalization data to make sure that the child is using the newly learned behavior in situations outside of the original teaching setting.

DATA COLLECTION CAN BE EASY AND ENJOYABLE

Don't let data collection be intimidating. True, it can feel overwhelming to have to track progress on a regular basis. In fact, you might feel that you can "just tell" when your student is making progress without having to take any data. But people aren't very good at monitoring progress without a good system. They tend to remember the best parts of a session—or the worst parts. Someone who didn't sleep well or isn't feeling well may tend to focus on the challenges. Likewise, someone who's in a great mood may report more positive outcomes. Also, people have a hard time seeing slow trends. For example, a teacher might think a child isn't making progress and therefore unnecessarily change an intervention, when the student is actually making slow and steady progress. Collecting regular and systematic data ensures that effective interventions will continue to be used and ineffective interventions will be modified.

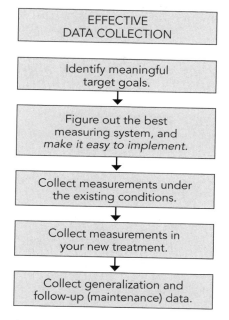

Components of effective data collection.

Now, let's talk about how to collect data without having it be burdensome. The last thing you want is piles of data that no one ever looks at. Teachers, interventionists, and parents are busy and don't have time to spend hours sorting out meaningless data points. That's why we discuss several ways to collect representative probes that don't interfere with the sessions but still guide you toward understanding a child's progress during intervention. No towers of papers, binders full of data sheets, or complicated graphs. In fact, the best data collection system is one that is not too hard or too inconvenient but still gives data that are representative and helpful in guiding your intervention and goals.

So how do you get started taking data? There are a few important components of effective data collection: 1) carefully identifying and defining a target goal, 2) figuring out the best way to measure the target goal you have identified, 3) collecting baseline measurements, 4) collecting measurements during intervention, 5) taking generalization and maintenance data, and 6) measuring treatment fidelity of implementation. Next, we go through these one by one. Because teachers or clinicians typically take data, the information is presented from that point of view. However, parents who are doing interventions may also find it useful to collect their own data.

*M**yth:* Data collection is burdensome.

*R**eality:* Data collection can be individualized to be both *easy* and *useful*.

Step 1: Identify and Define a Target Goal

The first step in a data collection process is to carefully identify and define a target goal. It is important that each goal be very, very specific. For example, if you are working on communication, don't pick "increase communication" as a goal. That's way too vague. Instead, break this general goal up into clearly defined parts, such as "increase the use of two-word utterances," "responds to peers' questions," or "initiates questions in a conversation with a peer." You can see that these goals will be a lot easier to take data on, because they are clearly defined, observable, and measureable. If you are working on social skills, identify a skill such as "increase percent of recess spent playing with peers," "responds verbally to peers," or "initiates play interactions with peers."

Identifying and defining a target goal

Vague target goal	Specific target goal
Increase communication.	Increase the correct use of past tense.
	Increase the ability to accurately recall and narrate personal past events.
	Increase the ability to maintain eye contact during social conversation.
Improve socialization skills.	Improve nonverbal pragmatic behavior. For example, improve keeping eye contact and staying with peers (not walking away) during a conversation.
	Increase the variety of appropriate initiations with peers.
	Increase question asking during social conversation.
Improve appropriate behavior.	Improve the ability to take turns during games.
	Learn to be flexible when losing a game.
	Sit nicely at the dinner table.

Again, you can measure these more effectively than "improves peer interactions."

Once you have an idea of what your goal is, be sure to define it in such a way that everyone who is observing the child agrees on the goal. For instance, if you choose "decrease inappropriate behavior with siblings," it might be hard for different people to agree what constitutes "inappropriate behavior." Instead, strictly define inappropriate behavior as "kicking, hitting, and throwing items or screaming at." Being specific helps everyone identify what behavior counts as inappropriate.

The following examples illustrate how to identify and define target goals. Rose, Mason, and Julian are three children we worked with; as you meet them, put yourself in our shoes as we decided how to take data.

Rose's Goal

Rose is a 2-year-old girl who is nonverbal. For Rose, an appropriate goal is increasing her communication. Specifically, the goal is for Rose to increase her use of one-word utterances. This is an appropriate goal given that she is nonverbal. *Rose's goal: Increase the number and variety of expressive verbal one-word utterances or communicative attempts in response to a verbal model.* You can probably already imagine the columns on your data sheet: 1) correctly produced words, 2) correct attempts, 3) type of words, and 4) percentage of responses following a model. See how much clearer this will be? Instead of indicating that she is "saying more words," you will have a very clear idea of Rose's behavior. Remember, you don't have to collect data on every single response Rose makes. You just want to collect enough representative data to be sure that Rose is making progress toward her goal.

Mason's Goal

Mason is a 6-year-old boy in an inclusive elementary setting. He likes to spend his time alone and engaged in preferred activities, which involve fantasy characters and scripts that he has memorized from movies. Furthermore, Mason frequently runs away when nonpreferred games are introduced. For Mason an appropriate goal is to increase his social engagement with peers. Again, the goal needs to be measurable. *Mason's goal: Increase the length of time engaged consecutively in games and activities with peers.* What will you include on Mason's data sheet? You would most likely take data on 1) the number of different activities he plays (that are not his restricted fantasy-based activities), 2) the amount of time he spends engaged with peers (both total minutes and consecutive minutes), and 3) the number of different peers with whom he plays. Eventually, when he's spending all of his recesses with peers, you would assess the quality of his interactions, but these first three types of data are a good start toward evaluating his progress on engaging in activities that are interesting to his peers.

Julian's Goal

Julian is a 13-year-old boy who has trouble with social conversation. Although he answers questions from peers, he rarely asks questions, and therefore his social interactions feature long, awkward pauses and silences. He spends most of his school day alone, although he reports that he wants to have more friends. For Julian, appropriate goals are improving his social conversation and his social engagement with peers. *Julian's goal: Increase time spent engaged with peers at recess and the number of questions he asks during social conversations with his peers.* Your data sheet would most likely include 1) the percent of time he engages in activities with peers, 2) the number of different peers he interacts with, and 3) the number of questions he asks his peers. If you really want to get some good quality-of-life data, you might want to collect data on whether he is hanging out with friends more often outside the school setting.

Summary

The areas of concern have been turned into specific goals for all three children. In all cases, the goal is defined so that multiple people will be able to agree that the targeted behaviors are occurring or not occurring. In fact, a stranger who walked up to each of these children, not knowing them or their strengths and weaknesses at all, would also be able to agree that the appropriate behaviors were occurring or not occurring. This is actually called the "Stranger Test"! Make sure that your goals are specific and clear enough to pass the Stranger Test before beginning to collect the actual data. Again, when you are writing goals for PRT, make sure that you are not writing out narrow, arbitrary goals. Be sure to make the goals meaningful.

*M**yth:** Data are just a bunch of meaningless numbers.*

*R**eality:** Data can show socially meaningful gains that alter the lives of the child and the family.*

Step 2: Figure out How to Measure the Target Goal

The second step is to figure out the best way to measure the target goal. Certain methods are better suited to certain behaviors. Above all, the data need to capture the behavior effectively. Whenever possible, the method of data collection should be simple enough that the interventionists are able to collect data while doing the intervention. The following are some of the different ways to collect data.

Frequency (or event) recording counts the number of times the target behavior occurs in a period of time. It is good for recording behaviors with a clear starting and ending point, such as question asking, spitting, or turns taken during a board game. Frequency recording doesn't make sense when you're measuring a behavior that occurs for a length of time, such as peer interaction or appropriate toy play, or when the start and end differ, such as a tantrum.

Trial-by-trial recording measures a child's responses to an opportunity or prompt and translates the number into a percentage. A good example of when you might use trial-by-trial data is if you are teaching a child to label colors of his favorite item. Each time you ask, "What color is it?" and the child responds correctly, you can mark that on your data sheet. If the child responds with the incorrect color, you will also tally that. Then, after a representative number of trials, such as 10 or 20, you can calculate the percentage of correct responses. This method allows you to compare intervention

Measuring target goals

Method	Description	Example
Frequency (event) recording	Count the number of times the target behavior occurs during a period of time.	Question asking Appropriate commenting
Trial-by-trial recording	Measure the child's response to an opportunity or prompt and translate the number into a percentage.	First words Appropriate commenting
Duration recording	Measure how long a behavior occurs.	Tantrum Peer engagement
Interval recording	Measure the percentage of intervals the child engages in a behavior of interest.	Staying on topic in conversation Appropriate voice volume
Latency recording	Measure the length of time from a predetermined point in time until the onset of a behavior.	Appropriate behavior in community settings Staying on task during academics

with your baseline measures and also to assess whether the child's responses are better than chance. Again, trial-by-trial data notes the percentage of opportunities to which the child responds correctly.

Duration recording measures how long a behavior occurs. This is useful when a behavior has a length and a clearly defined start and end. For example, you could record how long a tantrum lasts so that you can measure whether tantrums are getting shorter or longer in response to intervention. An important type of duration recording is latency recording, which measures the length of time from a predetermined point in time until the onset of a behavior. For example, you could measure how long it takes a child to start doing her homework after she is told to do it. Latency recording is especially useful when you are teaching a child or adult with disruptive behavior to increase the amount of time spent in community settings. For example, if you are teaching a child or adult to go grocery shopping, but the

There are many great applications for data collection. You can use an electronic device like the one in this picture or simply a piece of paper and a pencil. The main point is that data collection is critical to evaluating and tweaking your Pivotal Response Treatment program and assessing child outcomes.

individual engages in disruptive behavior, you may want to collect data on how long the individual can engage in shopping before becoming disruptive. If your intervention is effective, you should see this latency decrease.

Interval recording measures the percentage of intervals during which the child engaged in the behavior of interest. Sometimes a behavior has duration, but measuring that duration doesn't make sense. For example, you might want to know how long a child played with peers during recess. However, this behavior might stop and start many times. Similarly, if you want to measure whether a child was on-task while completing homework, it isn't going to be feasible to time from the beginning to end of every on-task period. For this, you might want to use interval recording. If you're interested in how much of recess was spent with peers, you might divide a 5-minute recess period up into ten 30-second intervals. Check off any interval in which the child spent time with peers. If he played with peers in intervals 3, 4, 5, and 10, he spent approximately ⁴⁄₁₀ or 40% of the intervals engaged in social behavior with his peers.

Next, let's revisit Rose, Mason, and Julian and think about what data collection strategy makes sense for each of them.

*M*yth: There is only one type of data.

*R*eality: The type of data collected needs to be individualized in order to be meaningful for the child's goals.

Rose's Data

The right approach for a child with a goal like Rose's (increasing one-word utterances) would be trial-by-trial data, because the opportunities are discrete; that is, the idea is to see how Rose responds when someone uses PRT to model a word for her. Taking trial-by-trial data is easy! To work with Rose, just number a sheet of paper 1–20. The figure shows how her sheet might look. Every time Rose responds to a one-word model prompt, write down the word or attempt. Every time she doesn't respond, cross out the trial number. Now you have a great idea of what Rose is saying, if she's making attempts, and the percentage of trials to which she responds. If you take data like this for several days in a row, you can tell whether Rose is improving at responding to model prompts, staying the same, or getting worse.

Word	Attempt	Word	Attempt
1		11	
2		12	
3		13	
4		14	
5		15	
6		16	
7		17	
8		18	
9		19	
10		20	
Word diversity		Word diversity	
Percentage of correct responses		Percentage of correct responses	
Percentage of responses		Percentage of responses	
Overall responses		Overall responses	

Rose's sheet.

Remember to provide enough opportunities to get a good idea of how Rose is responding. And if the data collection is interfering with the flow of the interactions and you don't feel the data are representative, you can always record a session and score it later or have someone else collect the data. Also, if you are finding that the data are quite variable, that's okay. You can take a closer look to see if there is anything that may be causing the variability. Is she better with certain people? Does she respond differently on specific days of the week? (Mondays are challenging for lots of people!) Are her responses different across settings? The great thing about data is that they allow you to become a detective and develop the best programs for your students.

Just a note: You don't need to take data on every single trial, as long as the data are representative and are taken often enough that they give you the information you need to adjust an intervention program. For example, if a child has a tantrum a few times a week, you'll probably want to take data on every tantrum. But if you're working on prompting first words, collecting data every few days or weekly may be more feasible and just as representative as well as less disruptive and time consuming. But remember, schedule data collection often enough to have a representative idea of how your student is doing so that you can tweak the program if necessary or move on to a new goal if one is achieved.

*M*_yth:_ Data need to be recorded on every single trial.

*R*_eality:_ Data can be gathered in probes once a week or even once a month to show time-lapse gains on large goals.

Mason's Data

Mason's goal (increasing how long he plays with peers) is a good example of when it is perfectly fine to combine recording systems. For the number of different activities he plays and the number of different peers he plays with, an event recording system is fine. Be sure to keep the number of minutes constant across observation periods. For engagement with peers during games and activities, duration recording makes perfect sense. For example, start timing at the beginning of the game and note how long Mason is able to engage

Number of minutes with peers	Number of peers	Number of activities
Monday		
Tuesday		
Wednesday		
Thursday		
Friday		
Number of times the child went out with friends during the week		

Mason's sheet.

before running away. You could also use a duration recording system and see if the number of minutes that he plays with his peers increases over time. The figure shows how the data sheet for Mason could look.

Julian's Data

As with Mason, you'll want to use a combination of data recording systems to capture whether Julian is spending more time with his peers and asking more questions in social conversation. Because Julian tends to spend time with a few different groups of friends and with different activities, an interval recording system could be most effective. For example, you could monitor a 10-minute interval during lunch period, once a week. Be sure to alternate among the beginning, middle, and end of the lunch period and among days of the week, because different activities will be going on, such as eating at the lunch tables, sports activities, club meetings, and so forth. Because the number of questions asked is a discrete and instantaneous behavior, frequency recording is perfect to measure progress toward this goal. You could take ten 10-minute samples. When using frequency recording, it's important to record frequency over

Minute (+ if engaged, – if not)	# of questions asked	# of peers interacted
1		
2		
3		
4		
5		
6		
7		
8		
9		
10		
Number of peers the child interacted with		
Number of activities		
Percentage of intervals engaged		

Julian's sheet.

the same interval each time. It's meaningless to compare two questions to six questions if he asked the two questions in 2 minutes and the six questions in 30 minutes. Likewise, you can collect frequency data on the number of different peers he interacts with. Julian's data sheet might look like the one shown.

Step 3: Collecting Baseline Measurements

Before you begin intervention, it is crucial to collect data on how the child is doing *before* you start an intervention. This might seem counterintuitive: If you think something will work, why shouldn't you just start the intervention? However, if you don't take data on how the child does without the intervention (this is called baseline, or pretreatment, measurement), you can't tell if the intervention made a difference. Maybe the child just happened to improve on the day you started the intervention. Maybe the child's behavior was already getting better, and your intervention didn't actually have an effect. You want to be sure to collect baseline data for two reasons: 1) so you can tell if the intervention worked and, if it isn't working, change your intervention, and 2) so you don't waste time working on something if it's getting better on its own! Taking baseline data is easy; just measure the same thing you plan to measure during the intervention, but don't do the intervention yet. (Use the Measurement: Baseline and Responsiveness to Intervention Guide on pp. 16–17 to track the data.) And then take data on a few occasions before you start the intervention. If the child is improving before you start the intervention, you'll probably want to just keep an eye on that behavior and work on something else that isn't improving on its own. Remember, don't waste a child's time. Every minute counts!

Rose's Baseline

Because Rose is nonverbal, she may respond to 0% of the trials. It might sound silly, but again, you need to document her baseline. Otherwise, you won't be able to tell if the intervention worked.

Mason's Baseline

For Mason, the intervention will be incorporating preferred items into activities and games. You may find that your baseline indicates that he spends no time (0%) engaged with his peers during recess and doesn't engage in any of the activities his peers enjoy. Be sure to take data on several days to find out if the behavior is consistent.

Julian's Baseline

To understand how data recording works in Julian's situation, let's look at the real data for him. Julian's baseline was interesting. It showed that he tended to spend time at the lunch tables with his peers and had a consistent group of peers with whom he ate. However, during the unstructured periods of lunch, he generally roamed around the campus and sought out teachers to interact with. Because we learned that peer proximity was frequent at the lunch tables but completely nonexistent during the unstructured times, we knew we needed to target more areas during the unstructured times, whereas we only had to target social conversation (question asking) while he was at the lunch table.

> **Baseline Measurements**
>
> Measures the child's behavior without the intervention

He also asked no questions to his peers but asked an average of two appropriate questions per minute to the teachers. This baseline data showed us that we didn't need to teach him how to ask questions; we just needed to work with him on how to ask those great questions to his peers.

Summary

There are a couple of important things to remember about baseline data. Every once in a while, it's not going to be appropriate to systematically take baseline data. Let's say you are targeting aggressive behavior toward peers and siblings. Because you know of an evidence-based intervention to decrease aggressive behavior, it's not ethical to keep measuring this dangerous behavior just to get your baseline measurement. In situations like that, you should try to get records or notes from previous days to establish how much aggressive behavior typically occurs.

Again, remember that taking data systematically means keeping all the conditions the same from baseline to intervention! Suppose you ask Julian to have 10-minute conversations with his little brother at 10 p.m. at night for baseline, and then you ask him to have 10-minute conversations with his best friend at lunch during interventions. Now suppose the data during intervention show improvement. Unfortunately, you can't say the intervention is the reason why he's doing better during intervention. It could be that he likes his partner better or that he's able to stay awake! So make sure that everything is constant between baseline and intervention. It's perfectly fine to take data in different settings and situations; just make sure you collect data in each of those settings during all phases: baseline, intervention, generalization, and follow-up.

Measurements During Intervention

Measures the child's behavior during intervention

Step 4: Collecting Measurements During Intervention

You already know how to do this! It's exactly the same as taking baseline data but with the intervention implemented.

Step 5: Taking Generalization and Maintenance Data

You have identified and defined a target behavior, figured out the best way to measure it, collected baseline and intervention data, and found that your intervention worked. Hooray! But there's one important last step: Check whether the intervention generalized. Generalization means that your student still shows the gains even when conditions are changed from those in which the intervention was taught. Working in the natural environment, as you do in PRT, greatly increases generalization. You can examine lots of different types of generalization. For example, if you've been teaching Rose to respond to model prompts with one-word utterances using the toys in her playroom, you can take her to a friend's house and see how she responds with different stimulus materials. If Julian has been practicing his social conversation with one person, you can check for generalization by asking him to have a conversation with someone new. Similarly, if Mason has gotten good at playing preferred games with friends from class, try it out with friends at his after-school club and see whether there is generalization.

Generalization and Follow-Up Measure

- Measures whether the child's gains are being exhibited in other, nonintervention settings
- Measures whether the intervention gains are maintained over time (i.e., after the intervention is completed)

You'll also want to make sure that the gains are maintained over time. Some children lose behaviors over the summer or slip a little during a vacation, even if your goal was met. To make sure goals are maintained, you can use the same recording system you used during baseline and intervention. If the target behaviors have been maintained, great! If not, you may need to do a few booster sessions. Again, this valuable information learned through data collection will help you provide the best possible interventions for your student. Collecting data helps ensure you are truly monitoring whether the intervention works and assures you that you are making good decisions for the student.

Step 6: Measure Treatment Fidelity of Implementation

Finally, it is important to measure whether the treatment is being implemented correctly. You should periodically record data on whether intervention providers—clinicians, teachers, and parents—are implementing the intervention correctly and with a high degree of fidelity of implementa-

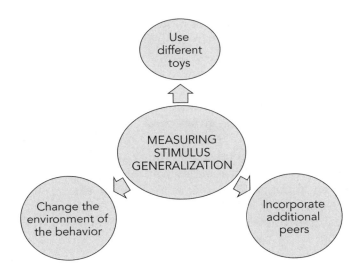

How to measure stimulus generalization.

tion. Fidelity of implementation simply means that the intervention is being implemented properly—the way it was intended. This is usually determined by research studies, and if the intervention isn't being implemented properly, it may not result in the desired behavior changes. You can use the interval recording procedures described above to track the fidelity of implementation. For example, you can record the intervention provider and then score 1- or 2-minute intervals for correct implementation of the procedures. You could document each category of PRT (e.g., using natural reinforcers, reinforcing attempts, using child choice) in each of the intervals, and see if they are being implemented correctly. This aspect of data collection helps everyone to remember that PRT is a serious business and not just playing and having fun with a child—although it is

Fidelity of Implementation

Measures whether treatment is being implemented correctly

that too! Here's the thing about PRT: It can be so much fun to implement that it is easy to forget that the point is to systematically implement a scientifically tested intervention and that the intervention must be implemented correctly for it to work. Collecting data on fidelity of implementation ensures that everyone involved is working correctly, which makes it more likely that the child will show important gains! If you want to be very sure about correctness, any intervention provider (including parents) can be certified (for more information, see http://www.koegelautism.com). The main point is that data allow you to assess whether the intervention is being done properly and whether the child is showing the gains you've hoped for.

*M*yth: Data are collected only on children's behaviors.

*R*eality: Data also need to be collected on adults' behaviors to ensure intervention is being implemented properly.

Ask Yourself

PARENTS & TEACHERS

1. Am I gathering data that are easy enough to obtain that I will do it regularly?
2. Am I gathering data at the proper interval (e.g., daily versus monthly)?
3. Am I gathering data that relate directly to the child's goals?
4. Am I gathering data that are meaningful with respect to socially meaningful gains for the child?

5. Are data being gathered on my behavior so I (and others who might question me) will be able to tell that I am implementing the procedures correctly?

6. Are data being gathered on other intervention providers' behaviors so I can tell whether they are implementing the procedures correctly?

References

Sources for the Science
Behind Pivotal Response Treatment

Albanese, A.L., San Miguel, S.K., & Koegel, R.L. (1995). Social support for families. In R.L. Koegel & L.K. Koegel (Eds.), *Teaching children with autism: Strategies for initiating positive interactions and improving learning opportunities* (pp. 95–104). Baltimore: Paul H. Brookes Publishing Co.

Baker-Ericzén, M.J., Stahmer A.C., & Burns, A. (2007). Child demographics associated with outcomes in a community-based Pivotal Response Training program. *Journal of Positive Behavior Interventions, 9*(1), 52–60.

Bandura, A. (1969). *Principles of behavior modification.* New York: Holt, Rinehart & Winston.

Barry, L.M., & Singer, G.H.S. (2002). Reducing maternal psychological distress after the NICU experience through journal writing. *Journal of Early Intervention, 24*(4), 287–297.

Beck, A.T., & Steer, R.A. (1987). *Manual for the revised Beck Depression Inventory.* San Antonio, TX: The Psychological Corporation.

Bernheimer, L.P., Gallimore, R., & Weisner, T. (1990). Ecocultural theory as a context for the individual family service plan. *Journal of Early Intervention, 14*(3), 219–233.

Bettelheim, B. (1967). *The empty fortress: Infantile autism and the birth of the self.* Oxford, England: Free Press of Glencoe.

Bijou, S.W., & Baer, D.M. (1966). Operant methods in child behavior and development. In W.K. Honig (Ed.), *Operant behavior: Areas of research and application* (pp. 718–789). New York: Appleton.

Bouma, R., & Schweitzer, R. (1990). The impact of chronic childhood illness on family stress: A comparison between autism and cystic fibrosis. *Journal of Clinical Psychology, 46*(6), 722–730.

Bristol, M.M., & Schopler, E. (1983). Stress and coping in families of autistic adolescents. In E. Schopler & G.B. Mesibov (Eds.), *Autism in Adolescents and Adults* (pp. 251–278). New York: Plenum Press.

Brookman-Frazee, L. (2004). Using parent/clinician partnerships in parent education programs for children with autism. *Journal of Positive Behavior Intervention, 6,* 195–213.

Bruinsma, Y. (2004). *Increases in joint attention behavior of eye gaze alternation to share enjoyment as a collateral effect of Pivotal Response Treatment for three children with autism.* Unpublished doctoral dissertation, University of California, Santa Barbara.

Bryson, S.E., Koegel, L.K., Koegel, R.L., Openden, D., Smith, I.M., & Nefdt, N. (2007). Large scale dissemination and community implementation of Pivotal Response Treatment: Program description and preliminary data. *Research and Practice for Persons with Severe Disabilities, 32*(2), 142–153.

Carr, E.G., Newsom, C., & Binkoff, J.A. (1976). Stimulus control of self-destructive behavior in a psychotic child. *Journal of Abnormal Child Psychology, 4,* 139–153.

Chambless, D.L., & Ollendick, T.H. (2001). Empirically supported psychological interventions: Controversies and evidence. *Annual Review of Psychology, 52,* 685–716.

Condouris, K., Meyer, E., & Tager-Flusberg, H. (2003). The relationship between standardized measures of language and measures of spontaneous speech in children with autism. *American Journal of Speech–Language Pathology, 12,* 349–358.

Dawson, M., Soulières, I., Gernsbacher, M.A., & Mottron, L. (2007). The level and nature of autistic intelligence. *Psychological Science, 18,* 657–662.

Dunlap, G. (1984). The influence of task variation and maintenance tasks on the learning and affect of autistic children. *Journal of Experimental Child Psychology, 37,* 41–64.

Dunlap, G., & Kern, L. (1996). Modifying instructional activities to promote desirable behavior: A conceptual and practical framework. *School Psychology Quarterly, 11,* 297–312.

Dunlap, G., & Koegel, R.L. (1980). Motivating autistic children through stimulus variation. *Journal of Applied Behavior Analysis, 13,* 619–627.

Dunlap, G., Koegel, R.L., & Kern, L. (1984). Continuity of treatment: Toilet training in multiple community settings. *Journal of the Association for the Severely Handicapped, 2,* 134–141.

Dunn, M., Flax, J., Sliwinski, M., & Aram, D. (1996). The use of spontaneous language measures as criteria for identifying children with specific language impairment: An attempt to reconcile clinical and research incongruence. *Journal of Speech and Hearing Research, 39,* 643–654.

Edelson, M.G. (2005). A car goes in the garage like a can of peas goes in the refrigerator: Do deficits in real-world knowledge affect the assessment of intelligence in individuals with autism? *Focus on Autism and Other Developmental Disabilities, 20,* 2–9.

Egel, A.L., Richman, G., & Koegel, R.L. (1981). Normal peer models and autistic children's learning. *Journal of Applied Behavior Analysis, 14*, 3–12.

Fuchs, L.S., & Fuchs, D. (1986). Effects of systematic formative evaluation: A meta-analysis. *Exceptional Children, 53*(3), 199–208.

Gallimore, R., Weisner, T.S., Kaufman, S., & Bernheimer, L. (1989). The social construction of ecocultural niches: Family accommodation of developmentally delayed children. *American Journal of Mental Retardation, 94*(3), 216–230.

Gillett, J.N., & LeBlanc, L.A. (2007). Parent implemented natural language paradigm to increase language and play in children with autism. *Research in Autism Spectrum Disorders, 3*, 247–255.

Guess, D., Sailor, W., & Baer, D.M. (1978). Children with limited language. In R.L. Schiefelbusch (Ed.), *Language intervention strategies* (pp. 101–143). Baltimore: University Park Press.

Guess, D., Sailor, W., Rutherford, G., & Baer, D.M. (1968). An experimental analysis of linguistic development: The productive use of the plural morpheme. *Journal of Applied Behavior Analysis, 1*(4), 297–306.

Harper, C.B., Symon, J.B.G., & Frea, W.D. (2008). Recess is time-in: Using peers to improve social skills of children with autism. *Journal of Autism and Developmental Disorders, 38*, 815–826.

Harrower, J.K., & Dunlap, G. (2001). Including children with autism in general education classrooms. *Behavior Modification, 25*, 762–784.

Hewett, F.M. (1965). Teaching speech to an autistic child through operant conditioning. *American Journal of Orthopsychiatry, 35*(5), 927–936.

Hinton, L.M., & Kern, L. (1999). Increasing homework completion by incorporating student interests. *Journal of Positive Behavior Interventions, 1*(4), 231–234.

Holroyd, J. (1987). *Questionnaire on resources and stress for families with chronically ill or handicapped members.* Branboon, VT: Clinical Psychology.

Holroyd, J., & McArthur, D. (1976). Mental retardation and stress on the parents: A contrast between Down's syndrome and childhood autism. *American Journal of Mental Deficiency, 80*, 431–438.

Howard, J.S., Sparkman, C.R., Cohen, H.G., Green, G., & Stanislaw, H. (2004). A comparison of intensive behavior analytic and eclectic treatments for young children with autism. *Research in Developmental Disabilities, 26*(4), 359–383.

Hung, D.W. (1977). Generalization of "curiosity" questioning behavior in autistic children. *Journal of Behavior Therapy and Experimental Psychiatry, 8*, 237–245.

Kanner, L. (1943). Autistic disturbances of affective contact. *Nervous Child, 2*, 217–250.

Kazdin, A.E. (1977). The influence of behavior preceding a reinforced response on behavior change in the classroom. *Journal of Applied Behavior Analysis, 10*, 299–310.

Kern, L., Vorndran, C.M., Hilt, A., Ringdahl, J.E., Adelman, B.E., & Dunlap, G. (1998). Choice as an intervention to improve behavior: A review of the literature. *Journal of Behavioral Education, 8,* 151–169.

Koegel, L.K., Camarata, S., Valdez-Menchaca, M., & Koegel, R.L. (1998). Setting generalization of question-asking by children with autism. *American Journal on Mental Retardation, 102,* 346–357.

Koegel, L.K., Carter, C.M., & Koegel, R.L. (2003). Teaching children with autism self-initiations as a pivotal response. *Topics in Language Disorders, 23*(2), 134–145.

Koegel, L.K., Koegel, R.L., Frea, W., & Green-Hopkins, I. (2003). Priming as a method of coordinating educational services for students with autism. *Language, Speech, and Hearing Services in Schools, 34*(3), 228–235.

Koegel, L.K., Koegel, R.L., Green-Hopkins, I., & Barnes, C.C. (2010). Brief report: Question-asking and collateral language acquisition in children with autism. *Journal of Autism and Developmental Disorders, 40*(4), 509–515. doi:10.1007/s10803-009-0896-z.

Koegel, L.K., Koegel, R.L., Hurley, C., & Frea, W.D. (1992). Improving social skills and disruptive behavior in children with autism through self-management. *Journal of Applied Behavior Analysis, 25*(2), 341–353.

Koegel, L.K., Koegel, R.L., Shoshan, Y., & McNerney, E. (1999). Pivotal response intervention II: Preliminary long-term outcome data. *Journal of the Association for Persons with Severe Handicaps, 24*(3), 186–198.

Koegel, L.K., Koegel, R.L., & Smith, A. (1997). Variables related to differences in standardized test outcomes for children with autism. *Journal of Autism and Developmental Disorders, 27,* 233–244.

Koegel, R.L., Bimbela, A., & Schreibman, L. (1996). Collateral effects of parent training on family interactions. *Journal of Autism and Developmental Disorders, 22,* 141–152.

Koegel, R.L., Camarata, S., Koegel, L.K., Ben-Tall, A., & Smith, A. (1998). Increasing speech intelligibility in children with autism. *Journal of Autism and Developmental Disorders, 28,* 241–251.

Koegel, R.L., Dyer, K., & Bell, L.K. (1987). The influence of child-preferred activities on autistic children's social behavior. *Journal of Applied Behavior Analysis, 20,* 243–252.

Koegel, R.L., & Egel, A.L. (1979). Motivating autistic children. *Journal of Abnormal Psychology, 88,* 4118–4126.

Koegel, R.L., Egel, A.L., & Williams, J. (1980). Behavioral contrast and generalization across settings in treatment of autistic children. *Journal of Experimental Child Psychology, 30,* 422–437.

Koegel, R.L., & Koegel, L.K. (1988). Generalized responsivity and pivotal behaviors. In R.H. Horner, G. Dunlap, & R.L. Koegel (Eds.), *Generalization and maintenance: Life-style changes in applied settings* (pp. 41–66). Baltimore: Paul H. Brookes Publishing Co.

Koegel, R.L., & Koegel, L.K. (1990). Extended reductions in stereo-typic behaviors through self-management in multiple community settings. *Journal of Applied Behavior Analysis, 1,* 119–127.

Koegel, R.L., & Koegel, L.K. (2006). *Pivotal Response Treatments for autism.* Baltimore: Paul H. Brookes Publishing Co.

Koegel, R.L., Koegel, L.K., & Camarata, S.M. (2010). Definitions of empirically supported treatment. *Journal of Autism and Developmental Disorders, 40*(4), 516–517.

Koegel, R.L., Koegel, L.K., & Surratt, A.V. (1992). Language intervention and disruptive behavior in preschool children with autism. *Journal of Autism and Developmental Disorders, 22*(2), 141–153.

Koegel, R.L., Koegel, L.K., Vernon, T.W., & Brookman-Frazee, L.I. (2010). Empirically supported Pivotal Response Treatment for children with autism spectrum disorders. In J.R. Weisz & A.E. Kazdin (Eds.), *Evidence-based psychotherapies for children and adolescents* (pp. 327–344). New York: Guilford Press.

Koegel, R.L., & Mentis, M. (1985). Motivation in childhood autism: Can they or won't they? *Journal of Child Psychology and Psychiatry, 26,* 185–191.

Koegel, R.L., O'Dell, M.C., & Dunlap, G. (1988). Producing speech use in nonverbal autistic children by reinforcing attempts. *Journal of Autism and Developmental Disorders, 18*(4), 525–538.

Koegel, R.L., O'Dell, M.C., & Koegel, L.K. (1987). A natural language paradigm for teaching non-verbal autistic children. *Journal of Autism and Developmental Disorders, 17,* 187–199.

Koegel, R.L., & Rincover, A. (1974). Treatment of psychotic children in a classroom environment: I. Learning in a large group. *Journal of Applied Behavior Analysis, 7,* 49–55.

Koegel, R.L., Schreibman, L., Britten, K.R., Burke, J.C., & O'Neill, R.E. (1982). A comparison of parent training to direct child treatment. In R.L. Koegel, A. Rincover, & A.L. Egel (Eds.), *Educating and understanding autistic children* (pp. 260–279). San Diego: College-Hill Press.

Koegel, R.L., Schreibman, L., Loos, L.M., Dirlich-Wilhelm, H., Dunlap, G., Robbins, F.R., & Plienis, A.J. (1992). Consistent stress profiles in mothers of children with autism. *Journal of Autism and Developmental Disorders, 22*(2), 205–216.

Koegel, R.L., Schreibman, L., O'Neill, R.E., & Burke, J.C. (1983). Personality and family interaction characteristics of parents of autistic children. *Journal of Consulting and Clinical Psychology, 16,* 683–692.

Koegel, R.L., Shirotova, L., & Koegel, L.K. (2009a). Antecedent stimulus control: Using orienting cues to facilitate first-word acquisition for nonresponders with autism. *Behavioral Analyst. 32,* (2), 281–284.

Koegel, R.L., Shirotova, L., & Koegel, L.K. (2009b). Brief report: Using individualized orienting cues to facilitate first-word acquisition in non-responders with autism. *Journal of Autism and Developmental Disorders, 39* (11), 1587–1592.

Koegel, R.L., Symon, J.B.G., & Koegel, L.K. (2002). Parent education for families of children with autism living in geographically distant areas. *Journal of Positive Behavior Interventions, 4*(2), 88–103.

Koegel, R.L., & Traphagen, J. (1982). Selection of initial words for speech training with nonverbal children. In R.L. Koegel, A. Rincover, & A.L. Egel (Eds.), *Educating and understanding autistic children* (pp. 65–77). San Diego: College-Hill Press.

Koegel, R.L., Vernon, T., & Koegel, L.K. (2009). Improving social initiations in young children with autism using reinforcers with embedded social interactions. *Journal of Autism and Developmental Disorders, 29*(9), 1240–1251.

Koegel, R.L., Werner, G.A., Vismara, L.A., & Koegel, L.K. (2005). The effectiveness of contextually supported play date interactions between children with autism and typically developing peers. *Research and Practice for Persons with Severe Disabilities, 30,* 93–102.

Koegel, R.L., & Williams, J. (1980). Direct vs. indirect response-reinforcer relationships in teaching autistic children. *Journal of Abnormal Child Psychology, 4,* 537–547.

Kuriakose, S., & Koegel, R.L. (2010, May). A longitudinal comparison of language assessments in young children with autism. In S. Kuriakose (Chair), *Cultural considerations for the assessment and influence of language in the treatment of individuals with developmental disabilities.* Symposium presented at the 36th Annual Convention of the Association for Behavior Analysis, San Antonio, TX.

Laski, K., Charlop-Christy, M.H., & Schreibman, L. (1988). Training parents to use the Natural Language Paradigm to increase their autistic children's speech. *Journal of Applied Behavior Analysis, 21*(4), 391–400.

Lovaas, O.I. (1977). *The autistic child: Language development through behavior modification.* New York: Irvington.

Lovaas, O.I. (1987). Behavioral treatment and normal education and intellectual functioning in young autistic children. *Journal of Consulting and Clinical Psychology, 55*(1), 3–9.

Lovaas, O.I., Berberich, J.P., Perloff, B.F., & Schaeffer, B. (1966). Acquisition of initiative speech in schizophrenic children. *Science, 151,* 705–707.

Lovaas, O.I., Koegel, R.L., Simmons, J.Q., & Long, J.S. (1973). Some generalization and follow-up measures on autistic children in behavior therapy. *Journal of Applied Behavior Analysis, 6,* 131–166.

Lovaas, O.I., Schaeffer, B., & Simmons, J.Q. (1965). Building social behavior in autistic children by use of electric shock. *Journal of Experimental Research in Personality, 1*(2), 99–109.

McCubbin, H.I., McCubbin, M.A., Nevin, R., & Cauble, A.E. (1981). Coping Health Inventory for Parents (CHIP). In H.I. McCubbin,

A. Thompson, & M.A. McCubbin (Eds.), *Family assessment: Resiliency, coping, and adaptation: Inventories for research and practice* (pp. 407–453). Madison: University of Wisconsin Publishers.

Moes, D., Koegel, R.L., Schreibman, L., & Loos, L.M. (1992). Stress profiles for mothers and fathers of children with autism. *Psychological Reports, 71,* 1272–1274.

Mundy, P., & Newell, L. (2007). Attention, joint attention, and social cognition. *Current Directions in Psychological Science, 16,* 269–274.

Mundy, P., & Sigman, M. (2006). Joint attention, social competence and developmental psychopathology. In D. Cicchetti & D. Cohen (Eds.), *Developmental psychopathology: Theory and methods* (2nd ed., Vol. 1, pp. 79–108). Hoboken, NJ: Wiley.

National Autism Center (2009). *National standards report.* Randolph, MA: Author.

National Research Council (2001). *Educating children with autism.* Washington, DC: National Academy Press.

Nefdt, N., Koegel, R.L., Singer, G., & Gerber, M. (2010). The use of a self-directed learning program to provide introductory training in Pivotal Response Treatment to parents of children with autism. *Journal of Positive Behavior Intervention, 12*(1), 23–32.

Odom, S.L., Boyd, B.A., Hall, L.J., & Hume, K. (2010a). Erratum to: Evaluation of comprehensive treatment models for individuals with autism spectrum disorders. *Journal of Autism and Developmental Disorders, 40,* 437. doi:10.1007/s10803-009-0873-6.

Odom, S.L., Boyd, B. A., Hall, L.J., & Hume, K. (2010b). Evaluation of comprehensive treatment models for individuals with autism spectrum disorders. *Journal of Autism and Developmental Disorders 40,* 425–436, doi:10.1007/s10803-009-0825-1.

O'Neill, R. (1987). *Environmental interactions of normal children and children with autism.* Unpublished doctoral dissertation, University of California, Santa Barbara.

Owen-DeSchryver, J., Carr, E.G., Cale, S., & Blakeley-Smith, A. (2008). Promoting social interactions between students with autism spectrum disorders and their peers in inclusive school settings. *Focus on Autism and Other Developmental Disabilities, 23,* 15–28.

Pierce, K., & Schreibman, L. (1995). Increasing complex play in children with autism via peer-implemented Pivotal Response Training. *Journal of Applied Behavior Analysis, 28,* 285–295.

Pierce, K., & Schreibman, L. (1997). Multiple peer use of Pivotal Response Training social behaviors of classmates with autism: Results from trained and untrained peers. *Journal of Applied Behavior Analysis, 30,* 157–160.

Plienis, A.J., Robbins, F.R., & Dunlap, G. (1988). Parent adjustment and family stress as factors in behavioral parent training for young autistic children. *Journal of the Multihandicapped Person, 1,* 31–52.

Russo, D.C., & Koegel, R.L. (1977). A method for integrating an autistic child into a normal public school classroom. *Journal of Applied Behavior Analysis, 10,* 579–590.

Russo, D.C., Koegel, R.L., & Lovaas, O.I. (1978). Human vs. automated instruction of autistic children. *Journal of Abnormal Child Psychology, 6,* 189–201.

Safer, N., & Fleischman, S. (2005). How student progress monitoring improves instruction. *Educational Leadership, 62*(5), 81–84.

Schreibman, L., Kaneko, W., & Koegel, R.L. (1991). Positive affect of parents of autistic children: A comparison across two teaching techniques. *Behavior Therapy, 22,* 479–490.

Seligman, M.E.P., Klein, D.C., & Miller, W.R. (1976). Depression. In H. Leitenberg (Ed.), *Handbook of behavior modification* (pp. 168–210). New York: Appleton-Century-Crofts.

Seligman, M.E.P., & Maier, S.F. (1967). Failure to escape traumatic shock. *Journal of Experimental Psychology, 74,* 1–9.

Seligman, M.E.P., Maier, S.F., & Geer, J. (1968). The alleviation of learned helplessness in the dog. *Journal of Abnormal and Social Psychology, 73,* 256–262.

Sheinkopf, S., Mundy, P., Claussen, A., & Willoughby, J. (2004). Infant joint attention and 36 month behavioral outcome in cocaine exposed infant. *Development and Psychopathology, 16,* 273–293.

Sherer, M.R., & Schreibman, L. (2005). Individual behavioral profiles and predictors of treatment effectiveness for children with autism. *Journal of Consulting and Clinical Psychology, 73,* 1–14.

Simpson, R.L. (2005). Evidence-based practices and students with autism spectrum disorders. *Focus on Autism and Other Developmental Disabilities, 20*(3), 140–149.

Singer, G., Singer, J., & Horner, R. (1987). Using pretask requests to increase the probability of compliance for students with severe disabilities. *Journal of the Association for Persons with Severe Handicaps, 12*(4), 287–291.

Skinner, B.F. (1954). The science of learning and the art of teaching. *Harvard Educational Review, 24*(232), 86–97.

Skinner, B.F. (1986). Is it behaviorism? *Behavioral and Brain Sciences, 9,* 716.

Sloane, H.M., & MacAulay, B.D. (Eds.) (1968). *Operant procedures in remedial speech and language training.* Boston: Houghton Mifflin.

Smith, A., & Camarata, S. (1999). Increasing language intelligibility of children with autism within regular classroom settings using teacher implemented instruction. *Journal of Positive Behavior Intervention, 1,* 141–151.

Smith, I.M., Koegel, R.L., Koegel, L.K., Openden, D.A., Fossum, K.L., & Bryson, S.E. (2010). Effectiveness of a novel community-based early intervention model for children with autistic spectrum disorder. *American Journal on Intellectual and Developmental Disabilities, 115*(6), 504–523.

Stahmer, A.C. (1995). Teaching symbolic play to children with autism using Pivotal Response Training. *Journal of Autism and Developmental Disorders, 25,* 123–141.

Steiner, A.M. (2011). A strength-based approach to parent education for children with autism. *Journal of Positive Behavior Interventions, 13*(3), 178–190.

Strain, P.S., McGee, G., & Kohler, F.W. (2001). Inclusion of children with autism in early intervention: An examination of rationale, myths, and procedures. In M.J. Guralnick (Ed.), *Early childhood inclusion: Focus on change* (pp. 337–363). Baltimore: Paul H. Brookes Publishing Co.

Symon, J. (2005). Expanding interventions for children with autism: Parents as trainers. *Journal of Positive Behavior Interventions, 7*(3), 159–173.

Taylor, B.A., & Harris, S.L. (1995). Teaching children with autism to seek information: Acquisition of novel information and generalization of responding. *Journal of Applied Behavior Analysis, 28,* 3–14.

Thorp, D.M., Stahmer, A.C., & Schreibman, L. (1995). Effects of sociodramatic play training on children with autism. *Journal of Autism and Developmental Disorders, 25,* 265–282.

Travis, L., Sigman, M., & Ruskin, E. (2001). Links between social understanding and social behavior in verbally able children with autism. *Journal of Autism and Developmental Disorders, 31*(2), 119–130.

Twardosz, S., & Baer, D. (1973). Training two severely retarded adolescents to ask questions. *Journal of Applied Behavioral Analysis, 6*(4), 655–661.

Varni, J., Lovaas, O.I., Koegel, R.L., & Everett, N.L. (1979). An analysis of observational learning in autistic and normal children. *Journal of Abnormal Child Psychology, 7,* 31–43.

Vaughan Van Hecke, A., Mundy, P.C., Acra, C.F., Block, J.J., Delgado, C.E.F., Parlade, M.V., … Pomares, Y.B. (2007). Infant joint attention, temperament, and social competence in preschool children. *Child Development, 78,* 53–69.

Vismara, L.A., & Lyons, G.L. (2007). Using perseverative interests to elicit joint attention behaviors in young children with autism: Theoretical and clinical implications for understanding motivation. *Journal of Positive Behavior Interventions, 9*(4), 214–228.

Wetherby, A.M., & Prutting, C.A. (1984). Profiles of communicative and cognitive-social abilities in autistic children. *Journal of Speech and Hearing Research, 27*(3), 364–377.

Williams, J.A., Koegel, R.L., & Egel, A.L. (1981). Response-reinforcer relationships and improved learning in autistic children. *Journal of Applied Behavior Analysis, 14,* 53–60.

Wolf, M.M., Risley, T.R., & Mees, H.L. (1964). Application of operant conditioning procedure to the behavior problems of an autistic child. *Behaviour Research and Therapy, 1,* 305–312.

Index

Tables, figures, and photos are indicated by *t*, *f*, and *p*, respectively.

BROOKES
PUBLISHING Co
www.brookespublishing.com